37 CATHOLIC CLASSROOM CRAFTS

...IN 20 MINUTES OR LESS!

37 Catholic Classroom Crafts

...in 20 minutes or less!

Nicole T. Woodard

TWENTY THIRD PUBLICATIONS 23rd

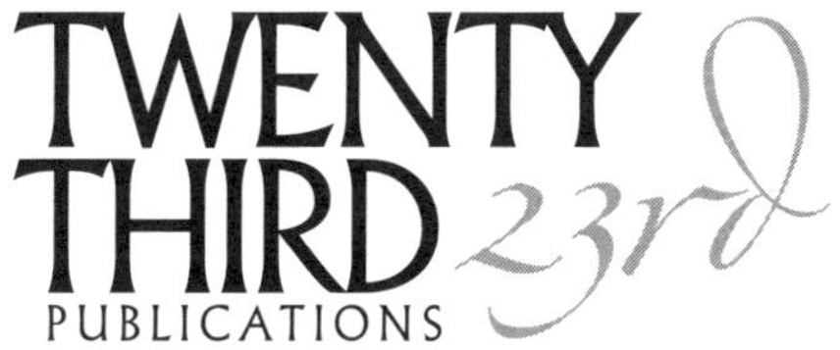

TWENTY-THIRD PUBLICATIONS
A Division of Bayard
One Montauk Avenue, Suite 200
New London, CT 06320
(860) 437-3012 or (800) 321-0411
www.23rdpublications.com

ISBN 978-1-58595-749-1

Library of Congress Catalog Card Number: 2009926109
Printed in the U.S.A.

CONTENTS

Ready...Set... *GO CRAFT!*

The countdown is on! Get set for an exciting adventure through the world of religious crafts. Together, we will take our children on a journey to the kingdom of God, through Bible verses and stories as well as fun games and activities, all done in twenty minutes or less (and costing mere pennies)!

As a longtime religious education teacher, I understand that many of us do not have extra time to schedule much beyond our course curriculum. Even if we do have time, it is often difficult to find fun, new, engaging, and tactile activities that can help our children experience the world of God.

So, with help from my students and other teachers just like you, I designed this book to do three primary things:

1. Prepare quick and easy crafts that can be created in the classroom in twenty minutes or less.
2. Create inexpensive crafts that generate learning and fun. (All the crafts can be done for pennies; we all know that religious education teachers spend much of their own money on supplies.)
3. Utilize easily accessible materials that can be found in your home and around your neighborhood.

This book also contains a companion CD with color images, worksheets, and cutouts that can easily be printed at your leisure. You will also find many hints and tips that will help get you organized and ready to do some crafting fun!

This book was created with a deep faith and love for God, which has shown me the ever-abundant beauty in all that we do and experience. My hope is that it enriches the journeys of all those who read it, and that they will come to see the true beauty of the world with childlike faith and wonder.

God bless you, and happy crafting!
Nicole T. Woodard

"I Am a Child of God" Paper Doll

What a wonderful feeling it is to know you belong! Whether we have dimples, freckles, or wear glasses, we are all God's children. God made each of us in his image, and yet we are all wonderfully different. Let's celebrate by creating a doll that looks just like us. It will be a reminder of all the wonderful things that make us special, and, most important, that God loves us.

See what love the Father has given us, that we should be called children of God.

(1 JOHN 3:1)

WHAT YOU NEED

Paper Doll worksheets
scissors
crayons or markers
brass paper fasteners (five for each boy doll, four for each girl doll)
hole punch
yarn (yellow, brown, black, and red)
glue sticks

PREPARATION

1. Make copies of boy and girl Paper Doll worksheets.
2. Begin cutting out the various parts of the doll's body. Each doll should have a head, two arms, one shirt, two legs for boy dolls or a skirt with legs attached for girl dolls.
3. Next, punch a hole in each body part where indicated below.

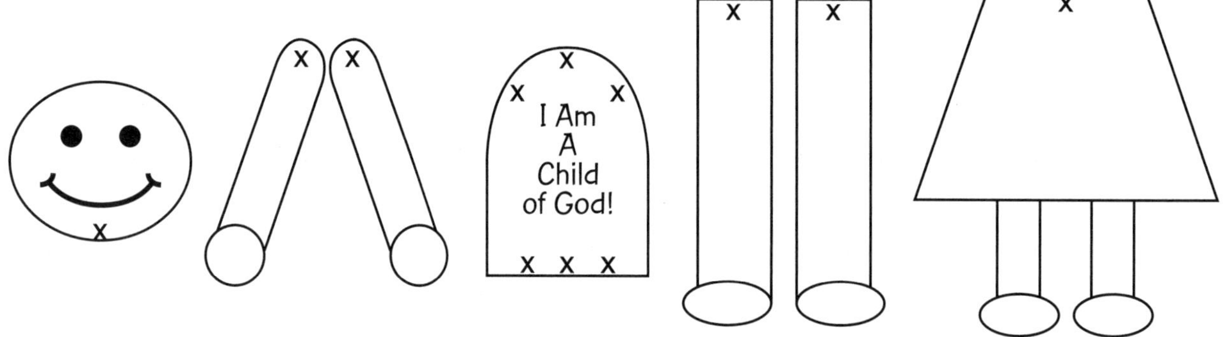

4. Using scissors, cut varying lengths of each color of yarn. Lengths should range from 4" to ½". The yarn will be used as the doll's hair.
5. Assemble kits.

   Each boy kit should include: one Paper Doll Boy worksheet, five brass fasteners

   Each girl kit should include: one Paper Doll Girl worksheet, four brass fasteners

CRAFT TIME

1. Give each child one pre-assembled kit that best resembles them.
2. If using black and white copies, color the dolls using crayons and markers.
3. Fasten the paper body parts to the shirt with the brass fasteners.
4. Using the yarn, glue the doll's hair on the head.
5. Have fun playing with your paper doll!

Paper Doll: Boy

Paper Doll: Girl

God Gave Me Five Senses Cube

God gives us all very special gifts. Some of these gifts help us live in the world around us. They are tasting, touching, seeing, smelling, and hearing. They help us appreciate other gifts that God has given us, like ice cream, furry animals, beautiful rainbows, fragrant flowers, and loud thunder in a storm. Let's practice using our five senses as we make our five senses cube.

Ever since the creation of the world his eternal power and divine nature, invisible though they are, have been understood and seen through the things he has made.

(ROMANS 1:20)

WHAT YOU NEED

Five Senses Cube Cutouts worksheet
hard stock paper or regular typing paper (for copying the cube outline)
scissors
glue stick
scratch-and-sniff stickers
small jingle bells
yarn or string cut to 5" (to tie bells onto cube)
sand paper, bubble wrap, velcro, strings of yarn, fuzzy or furry material, or anything with an obvious texture (1" x 1" square per child)
pretzels (five or six per child)
sandwich bag *(optional)*

PREPARATION

1. Make one copy of the Five Senses Cube Cutouts worksheet for each child. Cut out each cube outline.
2. Using the hole punch, punch two holes over the two Xs in the square with the ear in the upper right-hand corner.
3. Cut out one rainbow and one pretzel picture for each child
4. Cut or assemble the textured medium into 1" x 1" squares.
5. Cut scratch-and-sniff stickers into individual stickers.
6. Thread each piece of yarn/string through the jingle bells and tie to secure.
7. If using sandwich bags, place five or six pretzels in each bag.
8. Assemble kits.

   Each kit should include: one Five Senses Cube Cutouts worksheet, five or six pretzels, 1" x 1" textured item, one jingle bell, one piece of yarn/string, and one scratch-and-sniff sticker.

CRAFT TIME

1. Give each child one pre-assembled kit.
2. Fold the colored tabs back so that you can't see them.
3. Glue the pictures and textured item to the corresponding sense (i.e. rainbow/eyes, pretzel/mouth, textured item/hand, scratch-and-sniff sticker/nose).
4. Tie the jingle bell through the hole punches.
5. Fold each square along the dotted lines.
6. Fold each white tab along the dotted lines.
7. Turn cube outline over (to the blank side) so that only the glue tabs are showing.
8. Put glue on the white tabs that are labeled "glue." Glue each tab to the side of the cube that they are touching.
9. Place the pretzels inside the cube. Close the lid and you have your five senses cube!

Five Senses Cube Cutouts

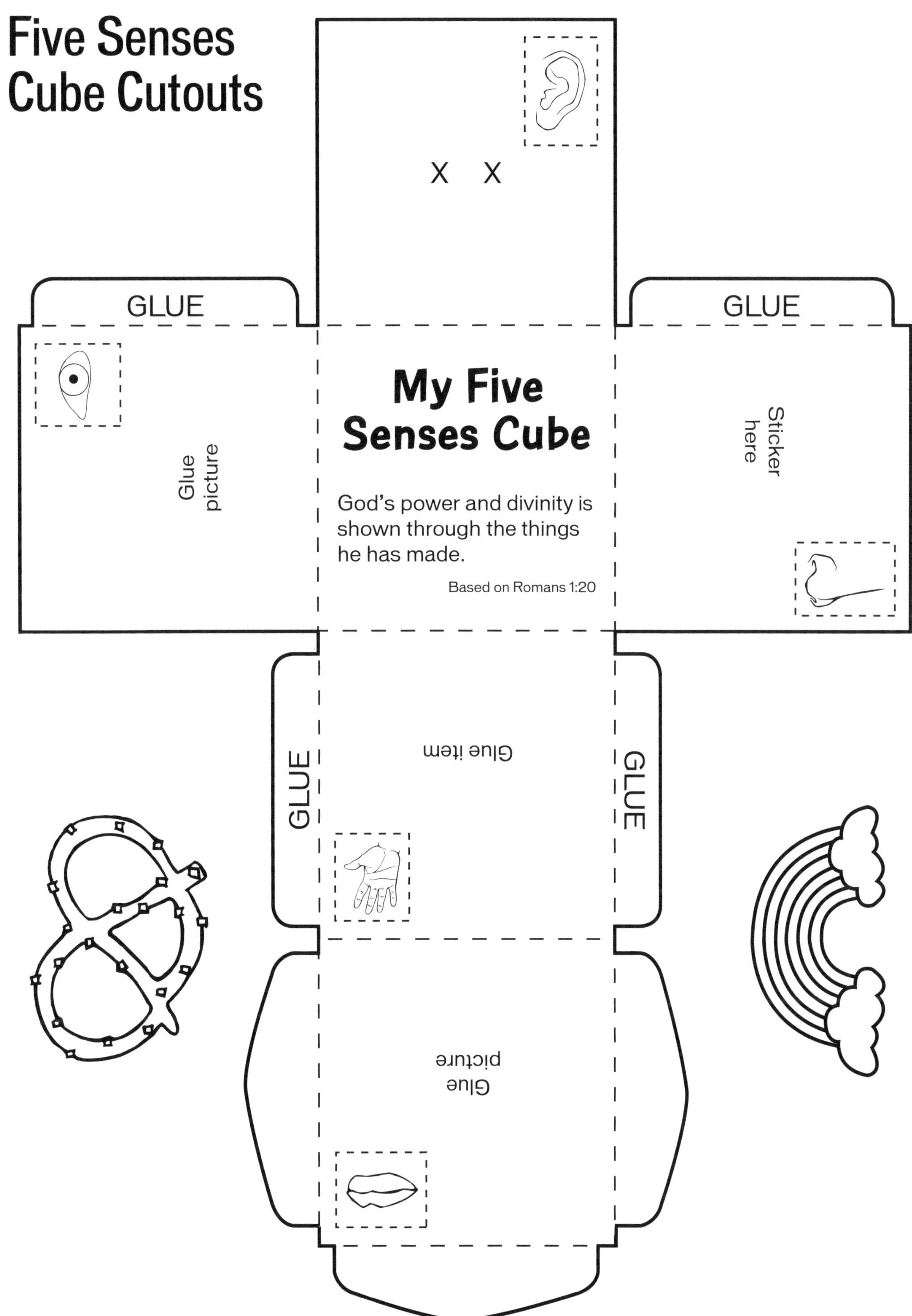

ACTIVITY #3

God Created the Earth Globe

What is the biggest present you ever received? Think really hard. I bet you didn't realize that the biggest present you ever received is the EARTH! The Earth is a huge present from God that bears all sorts of things like the gift of light, the gift of water, and the gift of land. He did all of this in six days. That's less than a week! The world is ours to enjoy and to love. In order to do that, we must take care of the Earth. When we do that, we show God our thanks and our love.

God called the dry land Earth,
and the waters that were gathered
together he called Seas.
And God saw that it was good.

(GENESIS 1:10)

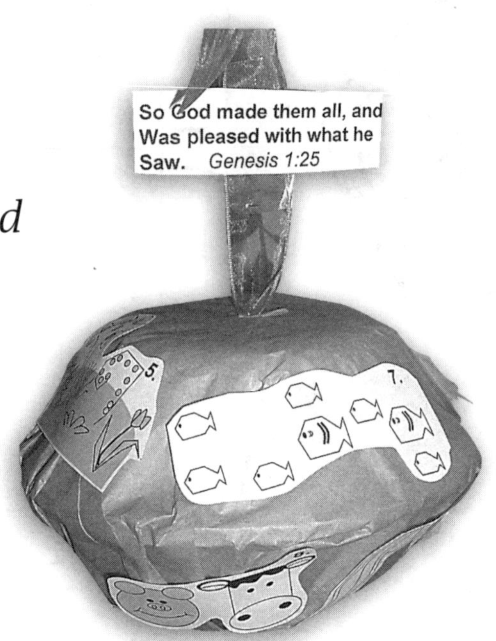

WHAT YOU NEED

God Created the Earth worksheet
disposable bowls (two per globe)
pencil or pen to pierce a hole in the bowl
yarn/string/ribbon 8" long
hot glue gun
blue tissue paper cut into 1" strips
scissors
glue stick
tape *(optional)*

PREPARATION

1. Poke a hole in the center of one of the bowls. Pull the 8" yarn/string/ribbon through the hole and fasten with tape or a knot. This will be the top half of your globe, and the yarn will help hang and display your creation.
2. Using your glue gun, carefully place glue around the rim of one bowl. Quickly, place the second bowl on top and seal to make a closed sphere.
3. Make copies of the God Created the Earth worksheet (one per child).
4. *Optional:* Using scissors, roughly cut out the pictures on the God Created the Earth worksheet. You should have nine pictures (numbered by the order that God created them) and one Bible verse per child. You may want to have the children do this step in class.
5. Cut tissue paper into 1" strips. The strips should be long enough to cover the sphere from top to bottom. Be sure to cut enough so that each child has enough to cover the entire sphere in blue.
6. Assemble kits.
   Each kit should include: one sphere with yarn, tissue paper strips, and one God Created the Earth worksheet.

Note: This craft goes very well with the Bible story in Genesis 1:1–19 and 1:20—2:3. You may want to read this story as the children glue their cutouts onto the globe.

CRAFT TIME

1. Hand out pre-assembled kits.
2. Begin by making a line of glue from the top of the globe to the bottom of the globe with the glue stick. Immediately place a piece of tissue paper on top of it. Press it to make sure it is firmly attached.
3. Repeat Step 2 until the entire globe is covered in tissue paper.
4. Cut out pictures from worksheet. If you did this during your preparation, go to Step 5.
5. As you read through the story in Genesis, glue the cutouts on the globe in the order that they occurred.
6. Finally, glue or tape the Bible verse to the yarn and hang your beautiful globe for the world to see!

God Created the Earth

9. 2. 4.

3. 5. 1.

6.

7. 8.

God made the wild animals of the earth and saw that it was good.

Based on Genesis 1:25

ACTIVITY #4

An Earthly Gift–Pinecone Bird Feeder

You know that God gave us the earth, the sea, the stars, and the sun. But did you know he also gave us the plants and animals which bring us so much happiness? We can enjoy the sweet smell of flowers growing in a garden, or we can chomp on a yummy apple that grew on a tree. We can run and skip with our favorite dog, or we can watch the cows graze in a meadow. God gave us all these wonderful things to feed us and make us happy, and, in turn, we take care of these gifts by enjoying them and making sure they are around for the world to enjoy. Let's create a craft in which we use a beautiful pinecone to feed and nourish our beautiful friends the birds. God will be so proud!

And God said,
"Let the earth bring forth
living creatures of every kind:
cattle and creeping things
and wild animals of the earth
of every kind." And it was so.

(GENESIS 1:24)

WHAT YOU NEED

pinecones (one per child)
12" long yarn or string
paper or plastic plate for peanut butter or shortening
peanut butter or shortening*
craft stick or plastic knife
bird seed
plastic sandwich bags
large plastic container

Note: Be sure to check for allergies. If a child is allergic to peanuts, shortening is a good alternative.

PREPARATION

1. Tie the yarn around the large end of the pinecone.
2. Fill a large plastic container with bird seed.
3. Assemble kits.
   Each kit should include: one pinecone, one plastic bag, one craft stick or plastic knife, and one paper plate.

CRAFT TIME

1. Hand out pre-assembled kits.
2. Place a scoop of peanut butter or shortening onto each paper plate.
3. Using the craft stick/plastic knife, smear peanut butter or shortening all over the pinecone.
4. Drop the pinecone into the plastic container of bird seed and roll around. Make sure the bird seed covers the majority of your pinecone.
5. Finally, hang your new bird feeder in a tree and enjoy watching God's creation!

If sending the children home with their bird feeders, you may want to place them in the plastic bags for safekeeping.

ACTIVITY #5

God Made All People Hand Imprint Picture

God made you, me, and all the people we see! The Bible says that God created all people in his image. Even though God created us in his image, we are still different is some very unique ways. For instance, we may have a head with two eyes, but our eyes are different colors. We may have hands and feet, but they are all different colors and sizes. In this activity we are going to study the similarities and differences in our hands and fingers. We'll examine the prints our hands and fingers make, all the time remembering that even though we may be different in some ways, we are alike because we are all created by God.

God gives to all people life and breath and all things.

(BASED ON ACTS OF THE APOSTLES 17:25)

WHAT YOU NEED

play dough (homemade play dough recipe* can be found on page 17)

resealable plastic bags

paper plates

craft stick or other apparatus for chiseling and drawing

glitter and/or confetti *(optional)*

One recipe is enough for three or four children

PREPARATION

1. Follow instructions for making homemade play dough.
2. Place ½-cup to ¾-cup portions of play dough into resealable plastic bags.
3. Assemble kits.
   Each kit should include: one bag of play dough, one paper plate, and one craft stick.

CRAFT TIME

1. Hand out pre-assembled kits.
2. Form the dough into a large round disc, big enough to fit your entire hand.
3. Have fun making designs on your dough and noticing how unique your handprint and fingerprints are.
4. Compare your handprint and fingerprints to other children in the class. Are their fingers longer or shorter than yours? Do their fingerprints look similar or different from your fingerprints? How many ways are your prints alike and different?
5. Try making fun pictures with your prints. Make a turkey out of your hand or even a caterpillar out of your thumbprints.
6. At the top of your imprint, chisel your name and other designs to make your own unique imprint. If you'd like, sprinkle with glitter and confetti, and let dry. Now you have your very own imprint to show just how unique God made you!

Scented Homemade Dough Recipe

INGREDIENTS

1 cup flour

¼ cup salt

¼ teaspoon cream of tartar

one package of unsweetened Kool-Aid mix (if making unscented, use food coloring)

1 cup hot water

DIRECTIONS

1. In a saucepan, mix together the flour, salt, cream of tartar, and Kool-Aid/food coloring.
2. Stirring constantly, add hot water and cook over medium heat for three minutes or until the mixture begins to form a ball.
3. Once the dough has formed a soft ball, remove from saucepan and knead for a few minutes on a counter covered with wax paper. Let cool.
4. Store dough in an airtight container when not in use.

ACTIVITY #6

Jesus the Good Shepherd Craft

Have you ever had something you loved so much that you always took really good care of it? Maybe it was a dog, a fish, or even a good friend. Well, a shepherd is a person who loves and cares over sheep all day and all night. Because the shepherd loves the sheep, he feeds them, watches them in hot and cold weather, looks for them when they are lost, and even fights off wild animals that might try to harm them. In that same way, Jesus is our good and loving Shepherd, and we are his sheep. He loves and protects us always. He is there to help us when we need him. Let's make a sheep to remind us that Jesus' love never fails.

I am the good shepherd. I know my own and my own know me, just as the Father knows me and I know the Father. And I lay down my life for the sheep.

(JOHN 10:14–15)

WHAT YOU NEED

Jesus the Good Shepherd worksheet
cotton balls
plastic bags *(optional)*
crayons, markers, and/or coloring pencils
glue

PREPARATION

1. Make one copy per child of the Jesus the Good Shepherd worksheet.
2. Gently fluff and pull apart the cotton balls so they closely resemble sheep's wool. This will also make your cotton balls go further.

CRAFT TIME

1. Give each child a copy of the worksheet.
2. Color the worksheet completely, excluding the body of the sheep.
3. Glue fluffed and stretched cotton balls onto the sheep's body and top of the head.
4. As the children work, read about Jesus the Good Shepherd in John 10:1–18 in a children's Bible.

Jesus the Good Shepherd

John 10:1–18

ACTIVITY #7

Noah's Ark Rainbow Craft

Rain, wind, wild animals, a big boat, a flood, and a good man all star in one of the most beloved stories of all time. Noah's Ark is a great story about a promise that God gave to a blessed man. Children and adults can appreciate the excitement and wonder in this story. Let's read together the story of Noah found in Genesis 6—9 and create a wonderful rainbow to remind us that God always keeps his promises.

Read Along

"And of every living thing, of all flesh, you shall bring two of every kind into the ark, to keep them alive with you; they shall be male and female. Of the birds according to their kinds, and of the animals according to their kinds, of every creeping thing of the ground according to its kind, two of every kind shall come in to you, to keep them alive. Also take with you every kind of food that is eaten, and store it up; and it shall serve as food for you and for them." Noah did this; he did all that God commanded him.

(GENESIS 6:19–22)

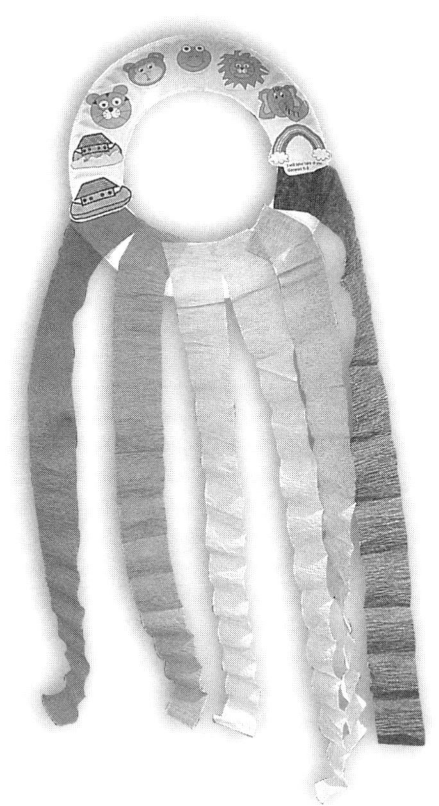

WHAT YOU NEED

Noah's Ark story
Noah's Ark worksheet
paper plates (one per child)
red, orange, yellow, green, blue, purple streamers
glue, tape, or stapler

PREPARATION

1. Cut a large hole in the center of each paper plate.
2. Cut streamers 18" long. Each child needs one streamer of each color.
3. Using the worksheet, cut out pictures along the dotted lines. Each child needs cutouts of one plain ark, one ark in the rain, two animals of each kind, and one rainbow.
4. Assemble kits by paper-clipping the items to the paper plate.
   Each kits should include: one streamer of each color (red, orange, yellow, green, blue, and purple) and one Noah's Ark worksheet.

CRAFT TIME

1. Read aloud the story of Noah's Ark. Hand out the pre-assembled kits.
2. At the bottom of the plate, have the children paste their streamers in the same order as in a rainbow (red, orange, yellow, green, blue, purple).
3. Review the story of Noah's Ark by gluing the cutouts in sequential order from left to right. What happened first? second? third? fourth? Noah built the ark; he gathered up the animals; the flood came; and then the rainbow came.
4. Have fun singing and dancing with these Noah Ark rainbows to fun gospel music! You can put them on your head as a fun hat, or take them outside to see the streamers blow in the wind!

The Story of Noah's Ark
Based on Genesis 6–9

A long time ago, the people of the Earth started behaving very badly. God saw that their ways were evil, and he became very sad that he had created them. "The only way to fix this," said the Lord, "is to remove them all from the Earth, for I am sorry that I ever made them."

But there was one man that was righteous and loved God with all his heart. That man was Noah. One day, God said to Noah, "The Earth is filled with so much evil that I must destroy it. I will bring a great flood, and everything on the Earth shall die. But because you are such a good man, and you have shown that you love me, I will make a promise to you to care for you and your descendents. You need to build an ark—large enough to hold two animals of every kind, male and female. Then you, your sons, and your sons' wives will board the boat with the animals. Also take every kind of food to be eaten and store it, and this will serve as food for you and them." Noah did as God told him.

Noah and his sons—Shem, Ham, and Japheth—all began working on the ark. When Noah and his sons finished the ark, God instructed them to go into the ark with the animals and food, as he had told them before. When the ark doors closed, God sent rain to the Earth that lasted forty days and forty nights. The waters rose so high that the ark rose up above the earth. All the mountains were covered with water, and all that had once lived died. Only Noah and those that were with him in the ark were left.

God remembered his promise to Noah, and he sent a great wind to blow over the Earth. Soon the waters subsided, and the ark came to rest on dry land. Noah opened a window and sent a dove out to see if the flood water had gone down enough for them to leave the boat. When the dove came back with an olive branch, Noah knew that the water was gone because plants were beginning to grow.

God said, "Noah, you may now leave the ark. May you and every living thing with you be fruitful and multiply on the Earth."

Noah's Ark

ACTIVITY #8

My Family's Love Wind Charm

God gives us each a very special gift that helps us to grow in faith and love. That special gift is our family. Our family can be our parents, grandparents, aunts, uncles, cousins, or friends. Family can be anyone who loves us and helps us to grow in love. One of the reasons why families are so special is because they are often the first place we learn how to love and accept our own similarities and differences. Let's celebrate our family's love by making a beautiful and unique wind charm, with our family members' names attached to the leaves. Now every time we sit outside and hear the beautiful jingle of our wind charm, we'll remember just how beautiful our families are too!

Live in love,
as Christ loved us.

(EPHESIANS 5:2)

WHAT YOU NEED

8" twig or stick

thin yarn, rope, fishing line, or dental floss

craft foam

jingle bells (five per child)

hole punch

scissors

PREPARATION

1. Cut five leaf shapes per child from your craft foam.
2. Punch a hole at the top and the bottom of the leaves.
3. Tie a 7" piece of string to the top of your leaves.
4. Using a shorter piece of string, tie a jingle bell to the other end of each leaf.
5. Tie a 12" piece of string to each end of the twig (for hanging the charm later).
6. Assemble kits.

   Each kit should include: one twig with hanger string and five leaves with bells and string attached.

CRAFT TIME

1. Write the names of your family members on each side of the leaves.
2. Tie the leaves evenly spaced from the stick.
3. Hang and enjoy!

ACTIVITY #9

My Stained Glass Church and Church Family Craft

Did you know that you have two families? You have the family that you live with at home and you have your church family. The church is your home in God's family. It's a place where we can pray, talk, eat, sing, and work together. Let's make a beautiful stained glass church to remind us of our beautiful church and our beautiful church family.

And I tell you,
you are Peter,
and on this rock
I will build my church,
and the gates of
Hades will not
prevail against it.

(MATTHEW 16:18)

WHAT YOU NEED

Church, Steeple, and Church Family worksheets
colored paper
legal size paper or larger (or regular size paper taped together to make a larger canvas)
tissue paper of various colors
glue
scissors
exacto knife *(optional)*

PREPARATION

1. Make copies of Church and Steeple worksheets onto colored paper. Make copies of the Church Family worksheet onto white paper. Each child will need one church, one steeple, one cross, and three church family cutouts.
2. Cut out the appropriate number of churches, steeples, and crosses.
3. Cut out the blackened windows, doors, and cross on the church and steeple. (***Tip:*** For quicker cutting, use an exacto knife.)
4. If pressed for time in class, you may choose to cut out the church family members from the Church Family worksheet along the dotted lines. Otherwise, skip this step and allow the children to cut them out in class.
5. Cut out small squares of tissue paper, large enough to be pasted on the inside of the church as windows. For the church windows the tissue should be approximately 3½" x 2". The tissue paper on the cross should be 1½" by 1". The round window on the steeple should have tissue paper cut to approximately 2" by 2". The door to the church on the steeple can be cut out and left uncovered.
6. Assemble kits.

   Each kit should include: one Church worksheet, one Steeple worksheet, one Church Family worksheet, and one legal size (or larger) paper.

CRAFT TIME

1. Hand out pre-assembled craft kits.
2. On the back side of the church (the side with no lines), sparingly place glue around the windows and cross. Place your tissue paper on top.
3. Repeat Step #2 on the steeple by placing tissue paper on the circular window.
4. Place glue on the "GLUE TAB" that is located on the steeple.
5. Place the outer ¾" of the left-hand side of the church over the tab to make one complete church.
6. Place glue on the back of the top half of the steeple and church and glue onto the top half of the large piece of paper.
7. Glue the church family in the free space on the large piece of paper.
8. You have a church! Lift up the bottom to see all the people inside. It would be fun to chant the well-known rhyme: "Here is the church; here is the steeple. Open the door and see all the people!"

Church

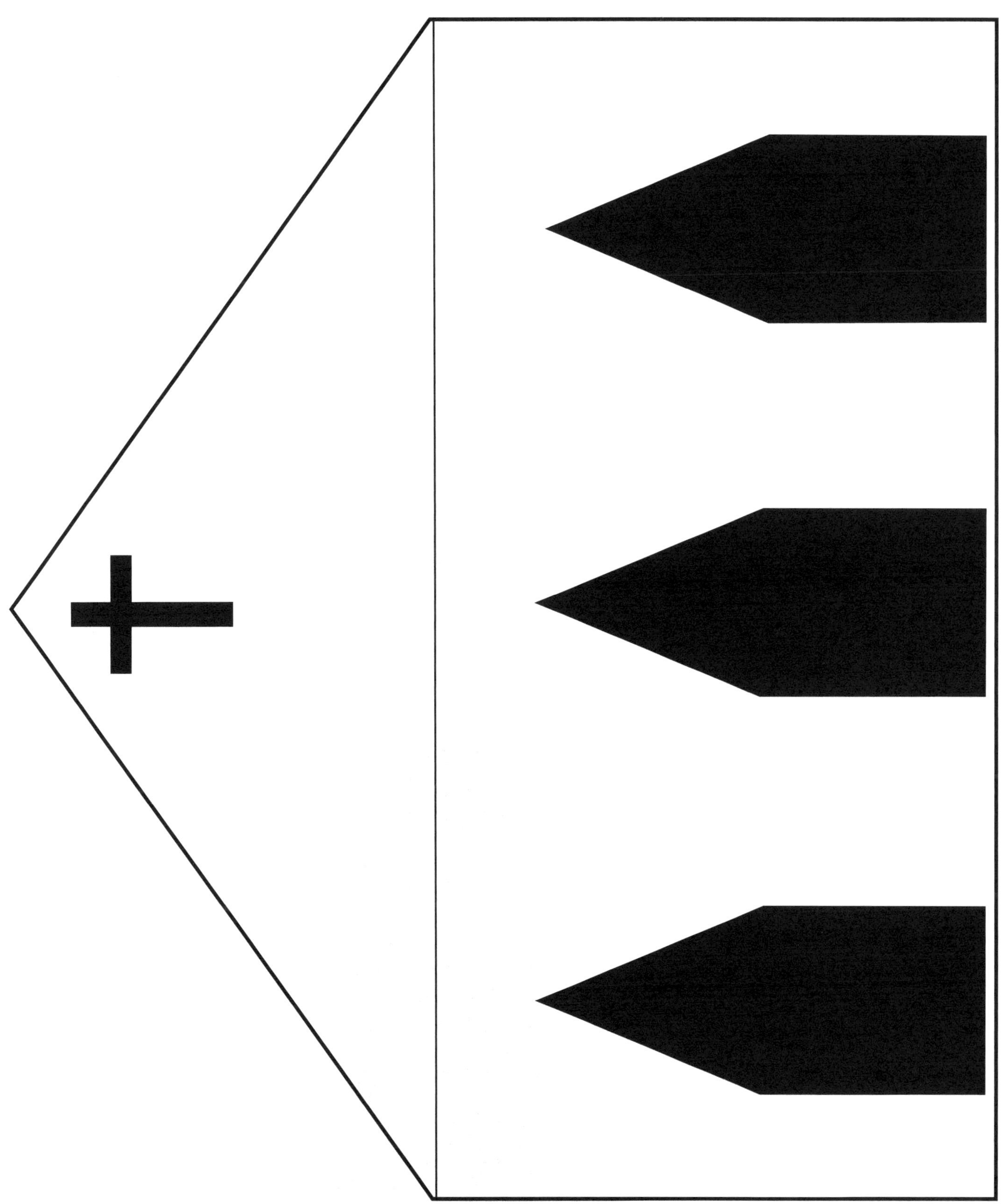

Steeple

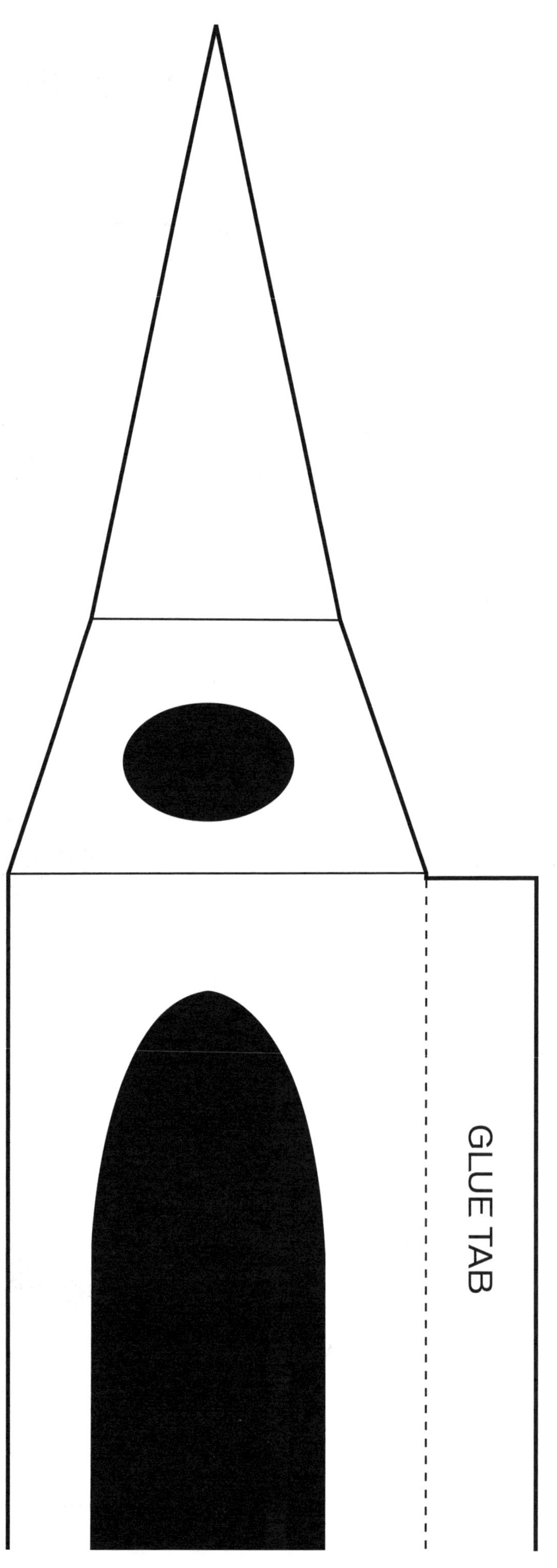

Church Family

ACTIVITY #10

The Holy Family Card Craft

Every family is different. Some families have a mom, a grandma, and one child. Other families have a dad, a mom, and three kids. Families consist of anyone who loves and cares for one another. The one thing that all families have in common is that they are all signs of God's love. Just like your family, the Holy Family, Mary, Joseph, and Jesus loved each other very much. They did things together like cooking, building things, and playing with each other. Let's make a card for our family to let them know just how much we love and care for them.

An angel came to Mary, who was to marry Joseph, and said, "Peace be with you. The Lord has greatly blessed you. You will give birth to a son and you will name him Jesus. He will be great, and he will be the Son of God." Mary said, "I am God's servant. May it happen as you have said."

(BASED ON LUKE 1:26–38)

WHAT YOU NEED

Holy Family worksheets (#1 and #2)
craft sticks (four per child)
glue
small pieces of straw, hay, or dried grass
crayons, markers, and pencils

PREPARATION

1. Make one copy per child of the Holy Family Worksheet #1.
2. Using worksheet #2 cut out the message that will later be pasted inside the card.
3. Assemble kits.
   Each kit should include: worksheet #1, one message cutout from worksheet #2, four craft sticks, and straw or grass.

CRAFT TIME

1. Hand out pre-assembled craft kits.
2. Fold worksheet #1 in half, so that the Holy Family is visible on the front.
3. Glue the craft sticks onto the dotted lines to form a house.
4. Glue grass or hay below the Holy Family.
5. Open the card and glue the message from worksheet #2 on the inside of the card.
6. Have the children write their name and their family name in the spaces provided.
7. Have fun decorating and coloring the card however you'd like! Give the card to your family and watch them smile!

Holy Family #1

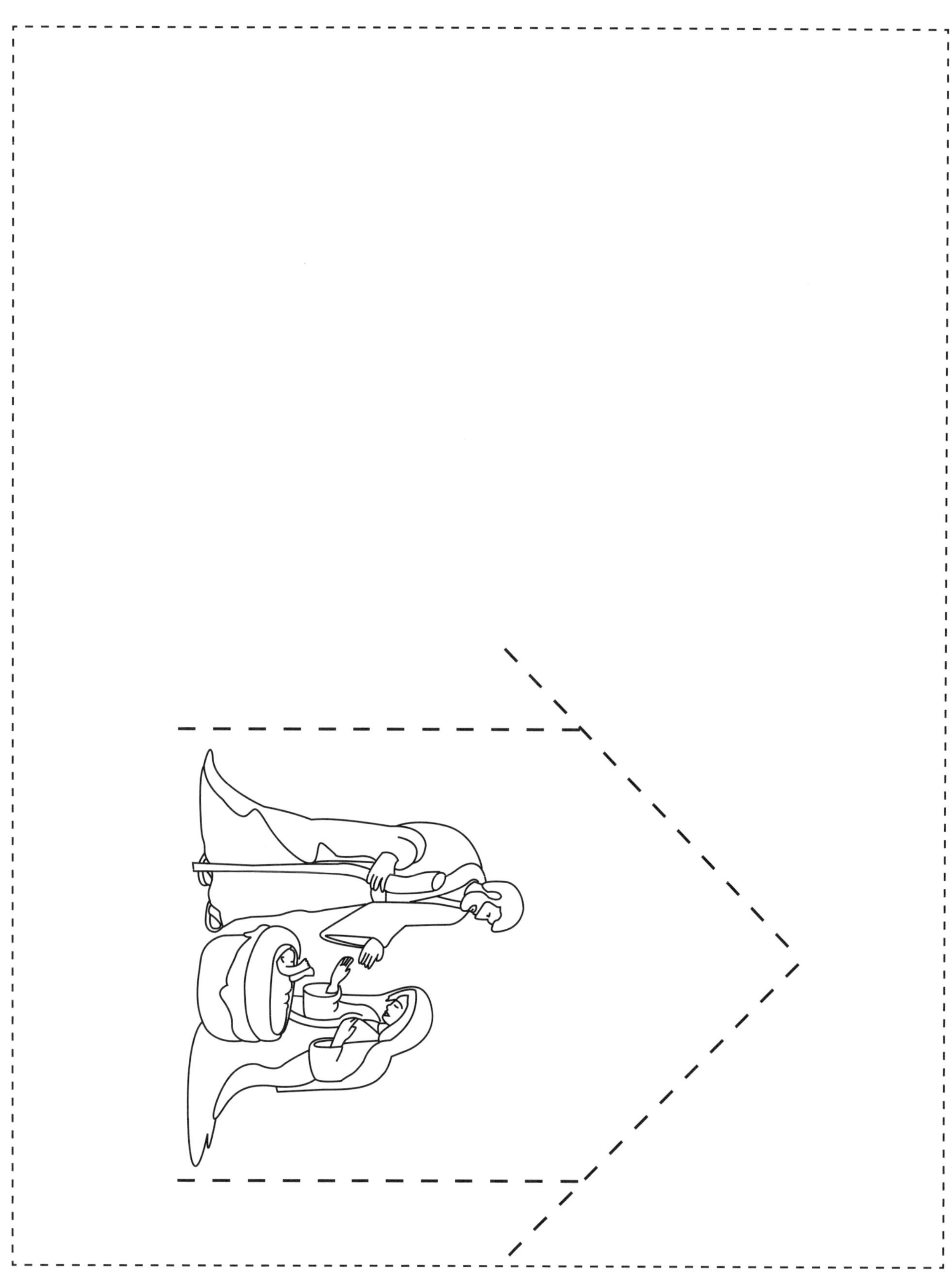

Holy Family #2

Dear ______________________,

Mary is the mother of Jesus.
Jesus is the Son of God.
Joseph cared for Mary and Jesus.

They are a family.
They love one another.
Just like I love you!

Love,

____

Jesus Makes Me Beautiful Butterfly Mobile

Have you ever witnessed the miraculous change of the wiggly, bumpy caterpillar into a graceful, beautiful butterfly? It is such a fantastic event! First, the eggs hatch and change into wiggly little caterpillars. The caterpillar eats and eats and eats until he changes into a big, fat caterpillar. Then, the caterpillar makes a gloppy mucus that changes the outside of his body into a hard shell, called a chrysalis. Soon an even bigger change takes place. The caterpillar cracks open his shell, and WHAM! he has turned into a beautiful butterfly. Jesus does the same thing for us. When we follow Jesus, we can turn our not-so-pretty qualities like selfishness and meanness into qualities like sharing, kindness, and caring. Try reading the story of Zacchaeus (Luke 19:1–8) and see how Jesus helped change a stingy tax collector into a kind and giving man. Then, try making this fun butterfly mobile that shows how Jesus can change the ordinary into the extraordinary!

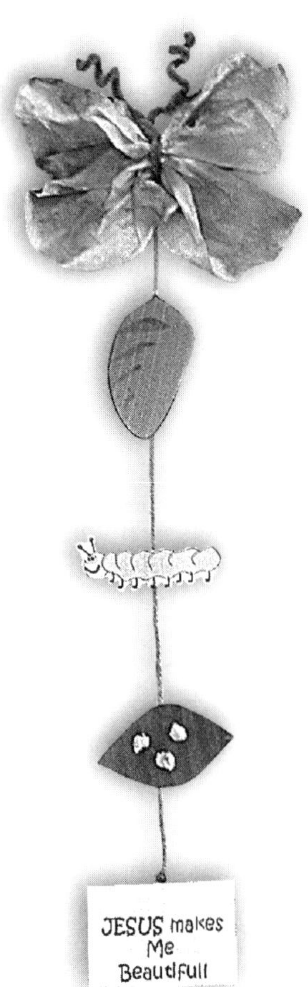

[Jesus] entered Jericho and was passing through it.
A man was there named Zacchaeus;
he was a chief tax-collector and was rich.
He was trying to see who Jesus was,
but on account of the crowd he could not,
because he was short in stature.
So he ran ahead and climbed a sycamore tree to see him,
because he was going to pass that way.
When Jesus came to the place,
he looked up and said to him,
"Zacchaeus, hurry and come down;
for I must stay at your house today."
So he hurried down and was happy to welcome him.
All who saw it began to grumble and said,
"He has gone to be the guest of one who is a sinner."
Zacchaeus stood there and said to the Lord,
"Look, half of my possessions, Lord, I will give to the poor;
and if I have defrauded anyone of anything,
I will pay back four times as much."

(LUKE 19:1–8)

WHAT YOU NEED

- Caterpillar Mobile worksheet
- coffee filters (two per child)
- markers
- water (spray bottle is helpful)
- pipe cleaners/chenille stems (one per child)
- colored paper* (dark green, light green, brown, yellow) *optional*
- yarn (28" long)
- glue, tape, or staples

If you do not use colored paper, use the black and white worksheets and the children can color the cutouts.

PREPARATION

1. Make copies of the attached worksheets (leaves/dark green, caterpillars/light green, chrysalis/ brown, Jesus makes me beautiful/white).

2. Begin by cutting out one leaf, one caterpillar, one chrysalis, and one Jesus makes me beautiful square for each child.
3. Cut one 28"-long string for each child.
4. Tear small strips of the yellow paper and roll them into pea-size balls. Make three per child.
5. Assemble kits.
   Each kit should include: one Caterpillar Mobile worksheet, three yellow paper balls, two coffee filters, one pipe cleaner, and one 28"-long string.

CRAFT TIME

1. Give each child one pre-assembled kit.
2. Using markers, color both coffee filters. Using various colors to make a unique butterfly.
3. While holding the filter up, spray it lightly with the water bottle. Watch how all the colors begin to spread and the design begins to change. Set the filters aside to dry.
4. Tape the Jesus makes me beautiful square to the bottom of the string.
5. Next, tape the leaf, caterpillar, and chrysalis in sequential order on the string, approximately 2" apart.
6. Glue the caterpillar eggs onto the leaf.
7. Bunch the filters in the middle and place one on top of the other to make the butterfly's body. Wrap the pipe cleaner around the filters, making sure to leave a little extra at the top for the antenna.
8. Fluff out your butterfly and tape 2" above the chrysalis. Now you have your butterfly mobile as a reminder of the beautiful changes Jesus can make in our lives!

Caterpillar Mobile

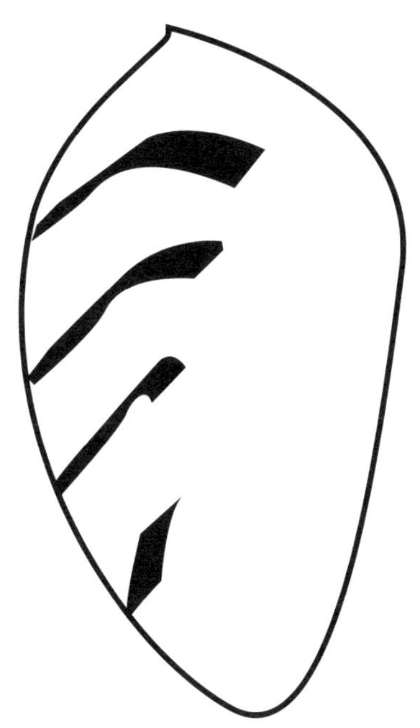

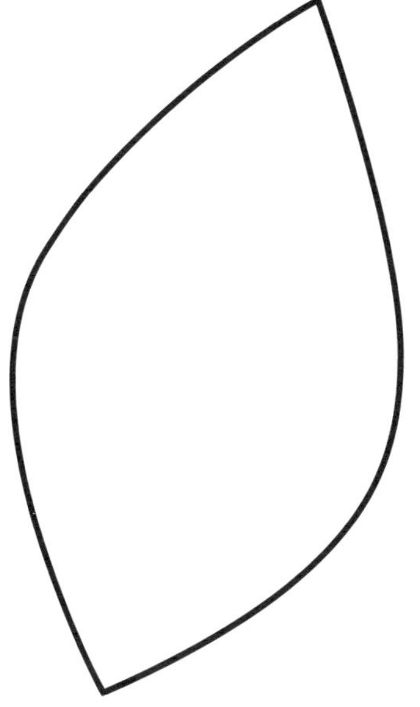

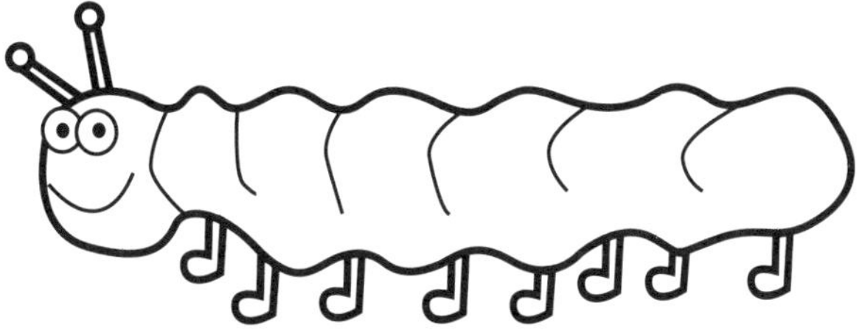

Jesus makes
me
beautiful!

ACTIVITY #12

Jesus Is My Teacher Clay Story

Did you know that Jesus was a teacher? Just like the teacher you have in school who teaches about math and reading, Jesus taught about the love of God. Many times, when he was trying to explain to people how much God loves them, he told stories. Today these stories can be found in the Bible. A fun way to recreate Bible stories is to actually build figures to illustrate the words. Let's read the story of the Loving Father (Luke 15:11–24) and build the characters with our minds and hands, which God so lovingly gave us!

Jesus went throughout Galilee, teaching in their synagogues and proclaiming the good news of the kingdom and curing every disease and every sickness among the people.

(MATTHEW 4:23)

WHAT YOU NEED

play dough or homemade dough (see page 17 for a recipe)

PREPARATION

1. Follow instructions for making homemade play dough.
2. Assemble kits by dividing clay into separate bags for each child.

CRAFT TIME

1. Begin craft time by reading the story of The Loving Father/The Prodigal Son (Luke 15:11–24).
2. After you have read the story once, begin the story again, this time creating figures along the way.
   a. 15:11 Separate the dough in half. With one half create three stick people (one father and two sons).
   b. 15:12 With the other half, make two balls to represent the property. Give one to each son.
   c. 15:13 Smash one ball and make it into bills and coins.
   d. 15:14 Destroy all the money and set it aside with the father and the other son.
   e. 15:15–19 Make little pigs out of the destroyed money.
   f. 15:20 Reunite the father and the son. Make them hug and kiss!
   g. 15:22 Using the old money and pigs, make shoes, a ring, a cloak, and yummy food for the feast!

DISCUSSION TIME

Let's talk about the story one more time. What do you remember from the story? Can you compare the father in the story to God? How are they the same? Have you ever done something that you shouldn't have? Do you think that God forgave you? What was your favorite part of the story? Why?

Prayer Rocks! Craft

Ever needed a little reminder to say your prayers? Sometimes we all could use a little help. With this functional craft, you can quickly and easily create a cute reminder to say your prayers every night and every morning. Why, they're so easy, you can make one for all the people you love.

Then when you call
upon me and come
and pray to me,
I will hear you.

(JEREMIAH 29:12)

WHAT YOU NEED

- Prayer Rocks! Poem worksheet
- three or four assorted 1" rocks
- square of scrap material (5" x 5")
- yarn or ribbon
- rubber bands
- scissors
- piece of paper (3" x 2.25")
- hole punch
- 2" clear tape

PREPARATION

1. Begin by cutting ½" slits around the edge of your scrap material. Cut them closer together for a more fringed look.
2. Make copies of the Prayer Rocks! Poem worksheet.
3. Cut out individual poems and cover with clear tape.
4. Punch a hole in the upper right-hand corner of your poem.
5. Assemble kits.
   Each kit should include: one material square, three or four rocks, ribbon, one rubber band, and one poem.

CRAFT TIME

1. Place your rocks in the center of your material.
2. Pull each of the four corners together to the center of the material. Secure them tightly around the rocks with a rubber band.
3. Pull a piece of your colored yarn through the hole in the poem. Securely tie the poem around the neck of your Prayer Rocks! craft.
4. Finish by adding more decorative yarn or ribbon around the rubber band.

Prayer Rocks! Poem

Prayer Rocks!
We are your prayer rocks,
And soon you will see
How nifty, how handy,
How helpful we can be.
Put us on your pillow
And at night you'll see,
When you lay your head down,
How lumpy we can be!
You'll suddenly remember
To say your nightly prayers
Because nobody wants to sleep
With rocks in their hair.
Put us on the floor
To do our next trick
And in the morning when you rise
Your feet will feel a prick.
"Praise Almighty God!"
You will happily say,
"Time to say my morning prayer
For this blessed day."

Prayer Rocks!
We are your prayer rocks,
And soon you will see
How nifty, how handy,
How helpful we can be.
Put us on your pillow
And at night you'll see,
When you lay your head down,
How lumpy we can be!
You'll suddenly remember
To say your nightly prayers
Because nobody wants to sleep
With rocks in their hair.
Put us on the floor
To do our next trick
And in the morning when you rise
Your feet will feel a prick.
"Praise Almighty God!"
You will happily say,
"Time to say my morning prayer
For this blessed day."

Prayer Rocks!
We are your prayer rocks,
And soon you will see
How nifty, how handy,
How helpful we can be.
Put us on your pillow
And at night you'll see,
When you lay your head down,
How lumpy we can be!
You'll suddenly remember
To say your nightly prayers
Because nobody wants to sleep
With rocks in their hair.
Put us on the floor
To do our next trick
And in the morning when you rise
Your feet will feel a prick.
"Praise Almighty God!"
You will happily say,
"Time to say my morning prayer
For this blessed day."

Prayer Rocks!
We are your prayer rocks,
And soon you will see
How nifty, how handy,
How helpful we can be.
Put us on your pillow
And at night you'll see,
When you lay your head down,
How lumpy we can be!
You'll suddenly remember
To say your nightly prayers
Because nobody wants to sleep
With rocks in their hair.
Put us on the floor
To do our next trick
And in the morning when you rise
Your feet will feel a prick.
"Praise Almighty God!"
You will happily say,
"Time to say my morning prayer
For this blessed day."

Prayer Rocks!
We are your prayer rocks,
And soon you will see
How nifty, how handy,
How helpful we can be.
Put us on your pillow
And at night you'll see,
When you lay your head down,
How lumpy we can be!
You'll suddenly remember
To say your nightly prayers
Because nobody wants to sleep
With rocks in their hair.
Put us on the floor
To do our next trick
And in the morning when you rise
Your feet will feel a prick.
"Praise Almighty God!"
You will happily say,
"Time to say my morning prayer
For this blessed day."

Prayer Rocks!
We are your prayer rocks,
And soon you will see
How nifty, how handy,
How helpful we can be.
Put us on your pillow
And at night you'll see,
When you lay your head down,
How lumpy we can be!
You'll suddenly remember
To say your nightly prayers
Because nobody wants to sleep
With rocks in their hair.
Put us on the floor
To do our next trick
And in the morning when you rise
Your feet will feel a prick.
"Praise Almighty God!"
You will happily say,
"Time to say my morning prayer
For this blessed day."

Prayer Rocks!
We are your prayer rocks,
And soon you will see
How nifty, how handy,
How helpful we can be.
Put us on your pillow
And at night you'll see,
When you lay your head down,
How lumpy we can be!
You'll suddenly remember
To say your nightly prayers
Because nobody wants to sleep
With rocks in their hair.
Put us on the floor
To do our next trick
And in the morning when you rise
Your feet will feel a prick.
"Praise Almighty God!"
You will happily say,
"Time to say my morning prayer
For this blessed day."

Prayer Rocks!
We are your prayer rocks,
And soon you will see
How nifty, how handy,
How helpful we can be.
Put us on your pillow
And at night you'll see,
When you lay your head down,
How lumpy we can be!
You'll suddenly remember
To say your nightly prayers
Because nobody wants to sleep
With rocks in their hair.
Put us on the floor
To do our next trick
And in the morning when you rise
Your feet will feel a prick.
"Praise Almighty God!"
You will happily say,
"Time to say my morning prayer
For this blessed day."

Prayer Rocks!
We are your prayer rocks,
And soon you will see
How nifty, how handy,
How helpful we can be.
Put us on your pillow
And at night you'll see,
When you lay your head down,
How lumpy we can be!
You'll suddenly remember
To say your nightly prayers
Because nobody wants to sleep
With rocks in their hair.
Put us on the floor
To do our next trick
And in the morning when you rise
Your feet will feel a prick.
"Praise Almighty God!"
You will happily say,
"Time to say my morning prayer
For this blessed day."

ACTIVITY #14

Jesus Is Always With Us Prayer Clock

Jesus is always with us! When we are in the bath, Jesus is there. At night when we go to sleep, Jesus is there. At school, while we learn, Jesus is there. Even though we can't see Jesus, we can always talk to him in our prayers. In this special way, we know that he is always with us, no matter what time of day. Let's make a clock together to show all the times we can talk with Jesus, in any place we like!

I desire, then, that in every place the men should pray, lifting up holy hands without anger or argument.

(1 TIMOTHY 2:8)

WHAT YOU NEED

Time to Pray worksheets
brass paper fasteners (one per clock)
hole punch

PREPARATION

1. Make one copy per child of the Time to Pray worksheets.
2. Punch a hole through the center of the clock.
3. Cut out one short hand and one long hand for each clock. Punch a small hole at the base of each hand.
4. Assemble kits.
   Each kit should include: one Time to Pray worksheet, one short arm, one long arm, and one brass paper fastener.

CRAFT TIME

1. Give each child one pre-assembled kit.
2. Thread the long and short arm through the brass faster.
3. Thread the brass fastener through the clock and fasten.
4. Have fun answering the questions that surround the clock and try these questions too:
   What time do you eat dinner? Is that a good time to pray?
   What time do you wake up in the morning? Is that a good time to pray?
   When is recess? Can you pray then?
   What about at lunch time?
   What time does school let out? Is that a time to say a thank-you prayer?

TIME TO PRAY!
12
1
2
3
4
5
6
7
8
9
10
11
Can I pray on the bus or on a plane?
Can I pray with friends?
Can I pray at church?
When can I pray?
Can I pray at school during lunch?
Can I pray while I play?

Time to Pray

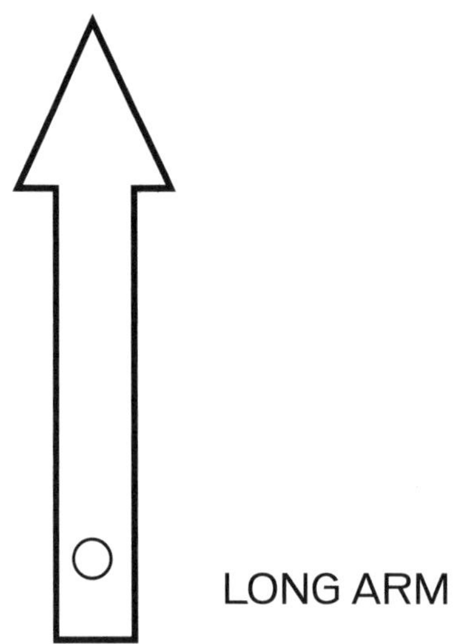

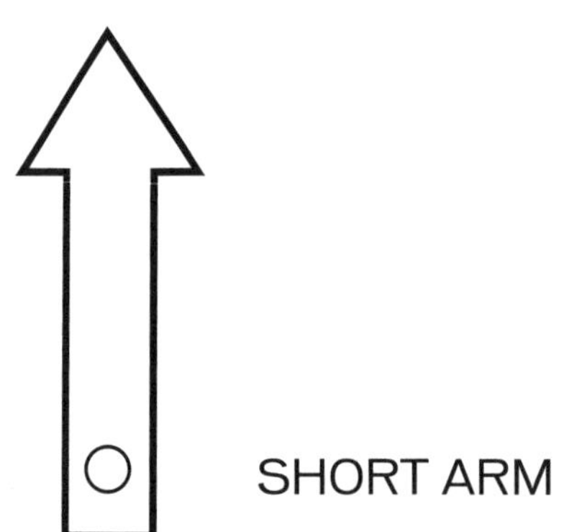

Jesus Is My Friend Bracelet

Who is our greatest friend, our biggest ally, and our strongest supporter? Jesus Christ Almighty! Let's rejoice in the fact that we have a friend who is there for us twenty-four hours a day. Now that's a powerful love! Let's make a bracelet to remind us of his enduring love. If you have time, make another and share the message with a friend.

I have called you friends, because I have made known to you everything that I have heard from my Father.

(JOHN 15:15)

WHAT YOU NEED

yarn or string
tape
"Let the Children Come to Me"
  Bible Verse worksheet
Fruit Loops™-type cereal
  (about thirty-six pieces per child)
aluminum foil
reinforcements
scissors
hole punch

PREPARATION

1. Cut yarn/string approximately 14" long.
2. Tie one piece of cereal to the end of the yarn/string to act as a stopper. If using yarn, also wrap a piece of tape around the opposite end. This will make it easier to push it through the cereal.
3. Begin making your cross charm. Cut 10" strips from your aluminum foil. Each strip should be ¼" to ½" thick.
4. Fold each strip in half lengthwise, and then in half again. Next, make the strip thinner by folding it in half width-wise.
5. Repeat Step 3 for the second strip of foil.
6. Form a cross by placing one strip over the other in the shape of a "t." Tightly wrap the strip that serves as the arms of the cross around the body of the cross.
7. Using your hole punch, punch a hole at the top of your cross. To ensure that the hole does not tear, place a reinforcement on top of your hole, folding over any excess.
8. Copy Bible Verse worksheet and cut out individual verses.
9. In the upper left-hand corner of each Bible verse, punch a hole. This will be another charm for the bracelet.
10. Assemble kits.
    Each kit should include: one Scripture charm, one aluminum cross, one yarn with stopper and taped end, and thirty-six pieces of cereal.

CRAFT TIME

1. Begin by threading one-third of the cereal on the yarn.
2. Thread the cross charm onto the yarn and follow with more cereal.
3. Next, add the Scripture charm to the bracelet.
4. Continue adding the cereal until the bracelet is finished.
5. Finish by tying the bracelet loosely around your wrist. Have fun sharing and eating your bracelet!

"Let the Children Come to Me" Bible Verse

"Let the children come to me, and do not stop them, because the kingdom of God belongs to such as these."
MARK 10:14

"Let the children come to me, and do not stop them, because the kingdom of God belongs to such as these."
MARK 10:14

"Let the children come to me, and do not stop them, because the kingdom of God belongs to such as these."
MARK 10:14

"Let the children come to me, and do not stop them, because the kingdom of God belongs to such as these."
MARK 10:14

"Let the children come to me, and do not stop them, because the kingdom of God belongs to such as these."
MARK 10:14

"Let the children come to me, and do not stop them, because the kingdom of God belongs to such as these."
MARK 10:14

"Let the children come to me, and do not stop them, because the kingdom of God belongs to such as these."
MARK 10:14

"Let the children come to me, and do not stop them, because the kingdom of God belongs to such as these."
MARK 10:14

"Let the children come to me, and do not stop them, because the kingdom of God belongs to such as these."
MARK 10:14

"Let the children come to me, and do not stop them, because the kingdom of God belongs to such as these."
MARK 10:14

Baptism–A New Life in Christ

One of the most spectacular wonders of the world is watching a seed come to life. If you stop and think about it, we are also like seeds. We are cared for by our loved ones and church, so that we can grow into beautiful human beings. Much like a seed, when we are baptized and water is poured over us, miracles occur as we become new people in Christ. Together, let's recreate the miracle of life by planting a seed. We'll soon see the beauty that lies in new life.

I have baptized you with water; but he will baptize you with the Holy Spirit.

(MARK 1:8)

WHAT YOU NEED

A New Life in Christ worksheet
dried lima beans
clear plastic cups (small)
1-quart plastic bags
soil/dirt
piece of paper (1½" x 4")
spray bottle with water
tape (*optional*, but 2" works well)

PREPARATION

1. Soak beans overnight.
2. Make copies of A New Life in Christ worksheet. Cut out individual instructions. These will help the parents understand the meaning of the craft, so that they will be able to assist their children once the craft goes home.
3. Tape the instructions to the cup. If using 2" clear tape, place the paper facedown on the tape, and tape to the side of the cup. The tape will act as lamination, protecting it from any water.
4. Fill the cup with soil.
5. Place the cup in the plastic bag. Seal it closed.

Note: The plastic bag has two benefits. It acts as an incubator to help the seed along its growth schedule, and it helps to catch any soil in case there are spills. Please do not skip this step.

CRAFT TIME

1. Give each child a plastic bag with soil and two lima beans.
2. Have the children separately place their lima beans in the cup, using their finger to gently push the bean into the soil. Be sure to instruct them to insert the bean at the edge of the cup, against the clear plastic wall. When the bean begins to grow, they can watch its progress.
3. Using the spray bottle, spray each plant with water.
4. Close the bag and write the child's name on top.
5. In six to eight days the children should see the full germination of their seeds!

A New Life in Christ

BAPTISM–A NEW LIFE IN CHRIST

Just as when we are baptized, pour water over your seed, so that it can grow and flower in the Holy Spirit. With continued loving care, watch your bean grow and take root, as you do in the love of God, your parents, and your church.

Instructions:

1. Keep me in the sun (5 hours a day).
2. Water me when I'm dry (keep slightly damp).
3. Watch me through the side of the cup (watch the roots as they develop).
4. Help me grow up to the sky (continue nurturing and caring for your new plant)!

BAPTISM–A NEW LIFE IN CHRIST

Just as when we are baptized, pour water over your seed, so that it can grow and flower in the Holy Spirit. With continued loving care, watch your bean grow and take root, as you do in the love of God, your parents, and your church.

Instructions:

1. Keep me in the sun (5 hours a day).
2. Water me when I'm dry (keep slightly damp).
3. Watch me through the side of the cup (watch the roots as they develop).
4. Help me grow up to the sky (continue nurturing and caring for your new plant)!

BAPTISM–A NEW LIFE IN CHRIST

Just as when we are baptized, pour water over your seed, so that it can grow and flower in the Holy Spirit. With continued loving care, watch your bean grow and take root, as you do in the love of God, your parents, and your church.

Instructions:

1. Keep me in the sun (5 hours a day).
2. Water me when I'm dry (keep slightly damp).
3. Watch me through the side of the cup (watch the roots as they develop).
4. Help me grow up to the sky (continue nurturing and caring for your new plant)!

BAPTISM–A NEW LIFE IN CHRIST

Just as when we are baptized, pour water over your seed, so that it can grow and flower in the Holy Spirit. With continued loving care, watch your bean grow and take root, as you do in the love of God, your parents, and your church.

Instructions:

1. Keep me in the sun (5 hours a day).
2. Water me when I'm dry (keep slightly damp).
3. Watch me through the side of the cup (watch the roots as they develop).
4. Help me grow up to the sky (continue nurturing and caring for your new plant)!

BAPTISM–A NEW LIFE IN CHRIST

Just as when we are baptized, pour water over your seed, so that it can grow and flower in the Holy Spirit. With continued loving care, watch your bean grow and take root, as you do in the love of God, your parents, and your church.

Instructions:

1. Keep me in the sun (5 hours a day).
2. Water me when I'm dry (keep slightly damp).
3. Watch me through the side of the cup (watch the roots as they develop).
4. Help me grow up to the sky (continue nurturing and caring for your new plant)!

BAPTISM–A NEW LIFE IN CHRIST

Just as when we are baptized, pour water over your seed, so that it can grow and flower in the Holy Spirit. With continued loving care, watch your bean grow and take root, as you do in the love of God, your parents, and your church.

Instructions:

1. Keep me in the sun (5 hours a day).
2. Water me when I'm dry (keep slightly damp).
3. Watch me through the side of the cup (watch the roots as they develop).
4. Help me grow up to the sky (continue nurturing and caring for your new plant)!

BAPTISM–A NEW LIFE IN CHRIST

Just as when we are baptized, pour water over your seed, so that it can grow and flower in the Holy Spirit. With continued loving care, watch your bean grow and take root, as you do in the love of God, your parents, and your church.

Instructions:

1. Keep me in the sun (5 hours a day).
2. Water me when I'm dry (keep slightly damp).
3. Watch me through the side of the cup (watch the roots as they develop).
4. Help me grow up to the sky (continue nurturing and caring for your new plant)!

BAPTISM–A NEW LIFE IN CHRIST

Just as when we are baptized, pour water over your seed, so that it can grow and flower in the Holy Spirit. With continued loving care, watch your bean grow and take root, as you do in the love of God, your parents, and your church.

Instructions:

1. Keep me in the sun (5 hours a day).
2. Water me when I'm dry (keep slightly damp).
3. Watch me through the side of the cup (watch the roots as they develop).
4. Help me grow up to the sky (continue nurturing and caring for your new plant)!

BAPTISM–A NEW LIFE IN CHRIST

Just as when we are baptized, pour water over your seed, so that it can grow and flower in the Holy Spirit. With continued loving care, watch your bean grow and take root, as you do in the love of God, your parents, and your church.

Instructions:

1. Keep me in the sun (5 hours a day).
2. Water me when I'm dry (keep slightly damp).
3. Watch me through the side of the cup (watch the roots as they develop).
4. Help me grow up to the sky (continue nurturing and caring for your new plant)!

Let's Go to Church–A Mass Activity

Let's go to church! This activity will be lots of fun as we learn about the order of Mass. We can act out the roles of the usher, lector, priest, altar server, and parishioners. We'll learn all about the miracles that happen every Sunday during Mass, as well as the significance of the different parts of Mass.

Note: There are two versions of this activity. The first is simple and inexpensive. However, if time and money permit, you may want to try version two, which allows the children to have an activity that they can bring home and enjoy over and over again.

I was glad when they said to me, "Let us go to the house of the Lord!"

(PSALMS 122:1)

WHAT YOU NEED: VERSION 1

Order of Mass worksheet
Church Layout worksheet
People of the Church Cutouts worksheet
glue stick
scissors

PREPARATION

1. Make one copy of each handout per child.
2. For younger children, or if time is an issue, cut out the individual pictures on the handout labeled "People of the Church Cutouts." You should have eleven pictures total per handout.

CRAFT TIME

1. Give each child a copy of the Church Layout and Order of Mass handouts.
2. Have the children paste the pictures in the appropriate places as you discuss the order of Mass, making sure they understand the various roles that individuals have in church, as well as the sacraments and rituals we follow every week.

WHAT YOU NEED: VERSION 2

Order of Mass worksheet
Church Layout worksheet
People of the Church Cutouts worksheet
scissors
lamination source*
velcro (self-adhesive) cut into ¼" x ¼" squares (you can also use non-adhesive velcro and adhere using a glue gun)

Note: You can use a laminating machine or laminating sheets. Some Christian bookstores and educational stores have in-house laminators for use at very economical prices.

PREPARATION

1. Make one copy of each of the three handouts per child.
2. Cut out the individual pictures on the handout labeled "People of the Church Cutouts."
3. Laminate one Empty Church handout for each child.
4. Next, laminate the individual pictures from the Cutout handout. Cut out each individual picture from the laminate.
5. Using your self-adhesive velcro tape, place the fuzzy side on each location noted by an "X" on Figure 1 on page 57.
6. Next, place the rough side of the Velcro on the back of each individual cutout.

7. On the front side of the three-person family, place the fuzzy side of the velcro in each location noted by an "X" on Figure 2 (see below). Do the same with the altar server and the usher. These will be used later to hold the gifts, cross, and offertory basket.

CRAFT TIME

1. Give each child a copy of the laminated Church Layout worksheet, eleven laminated pictures (placed in individual sandwich bags to keep little pieces together), and one photocopy of the Order of Mass worksheet.
2. Before Mass begins, have the children use the usher to seat the parishioners. The priest, altar servers, and lector can gather in the aisle before proceeding to the altar.
3. Continue to work through the order of Mass as indicated in the handout. Make sure they understand the various roles that each individual has in the church, as well as the sacraments and rituals we follow every week.

Figure 1

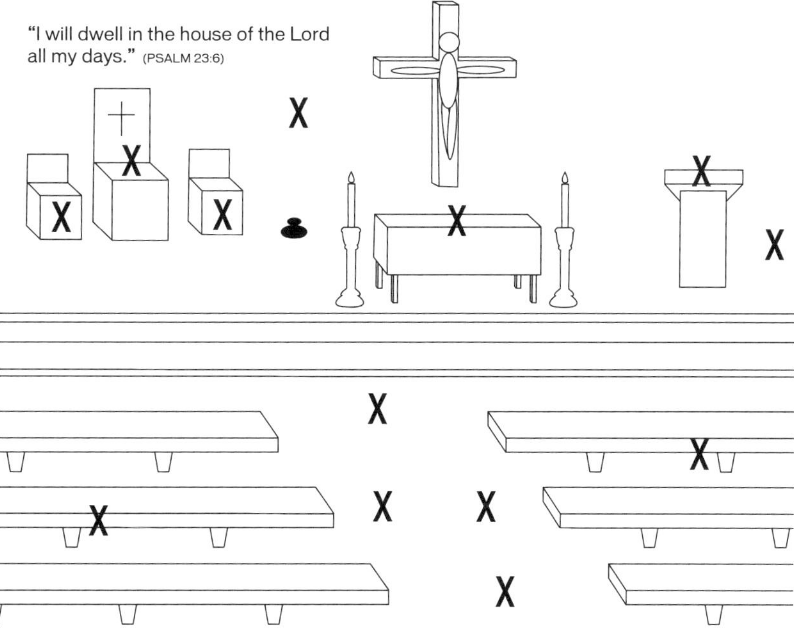

Figure 2

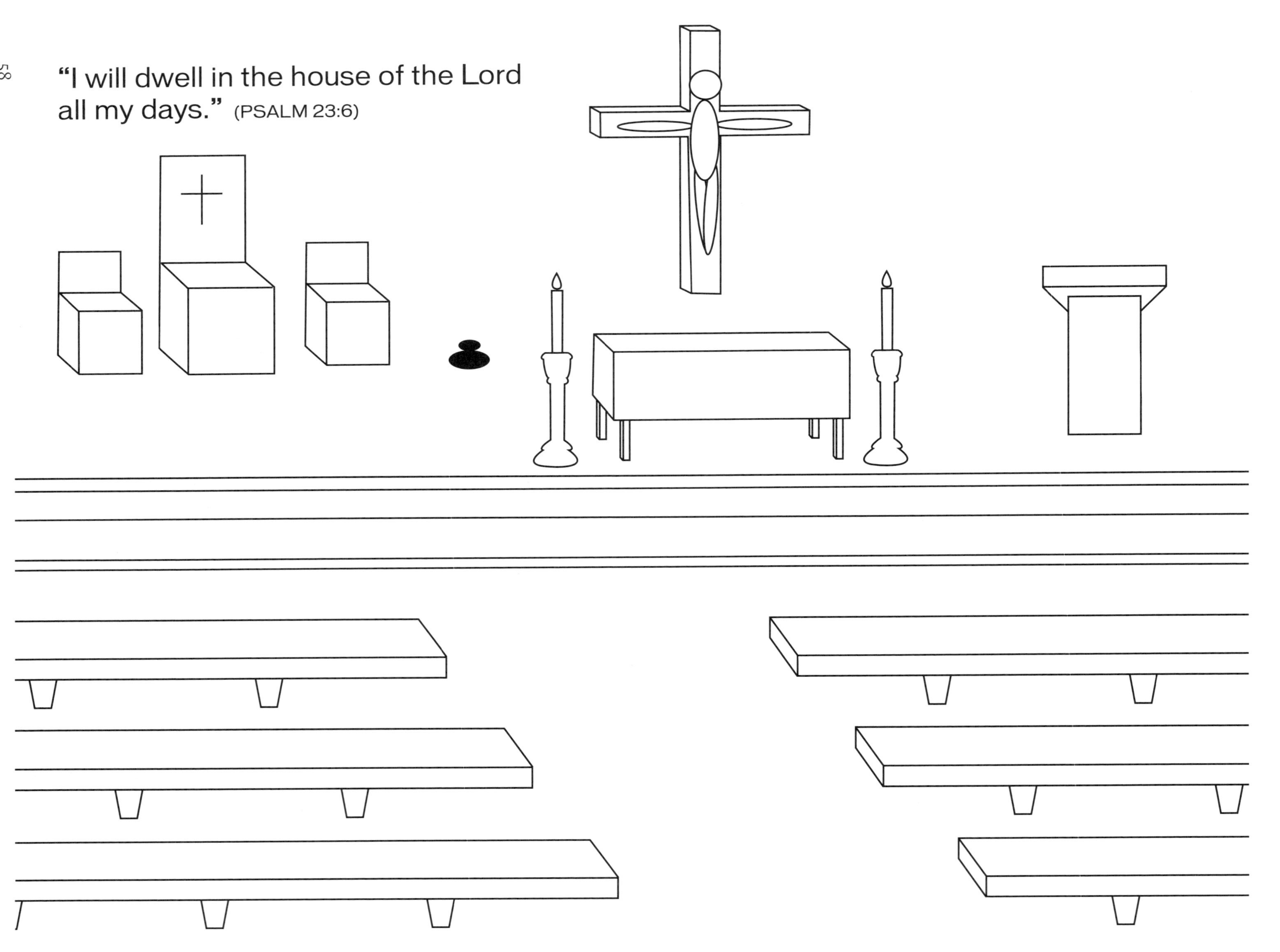
"I will dwell in the house of the Lord
all my days." (PSALM 23:6)

People of the Church Cutouts

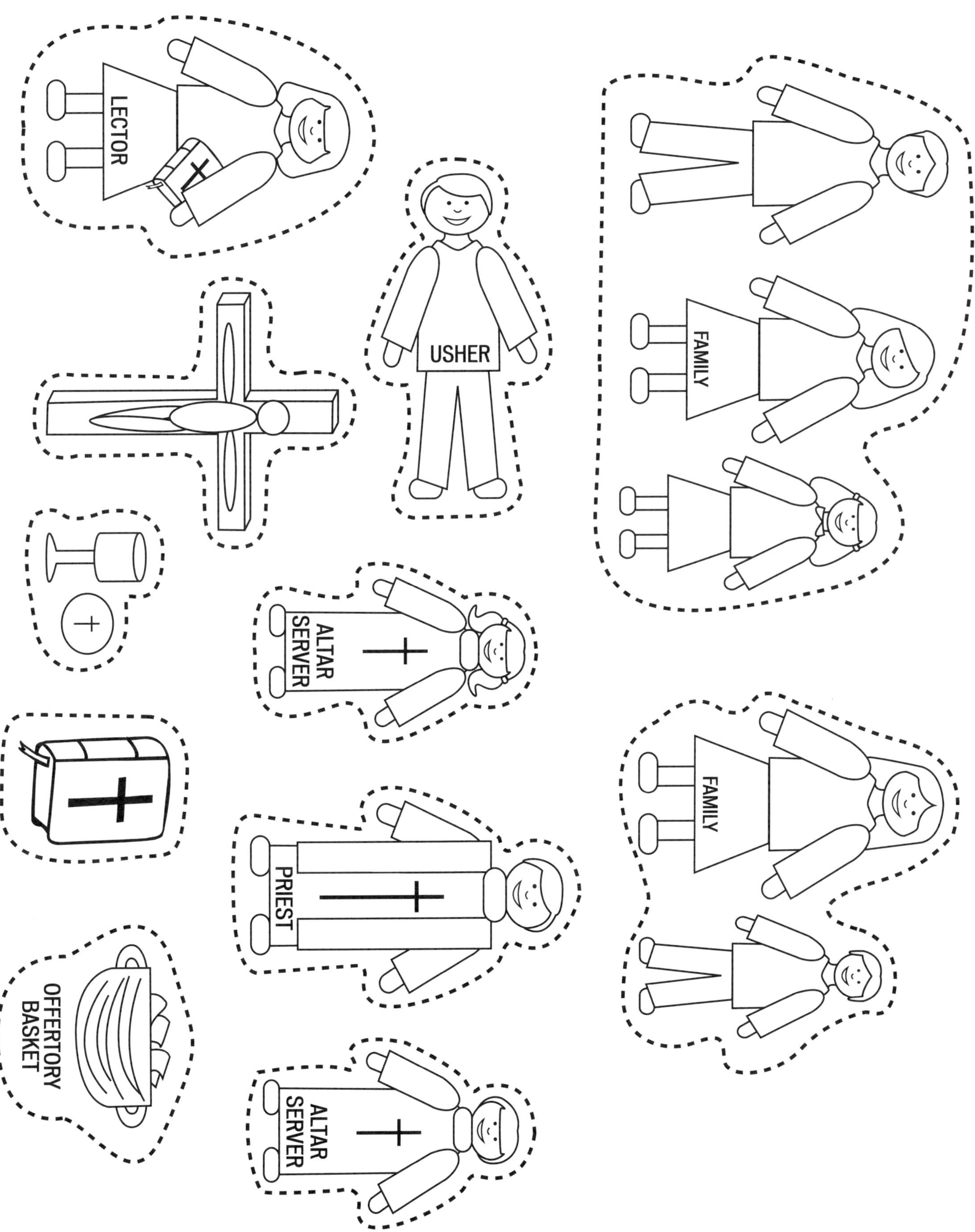

Order of Mass

SEATING: Who helps to seat the parishioners?

ENTRANCE: Who enters with the priest? What do they bring with them?

READINGS: Who reads the word of God?

GOSPEL: Who reads the Gospel?

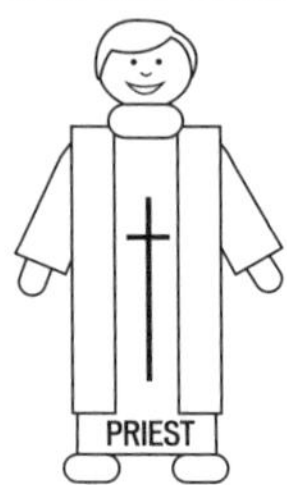

GIFTS: What are the gifts? Who brings them to the altar?

SIGN OF PEACE: What do we say during the sign of peace?

COMMUNION: What happens during Communion? Where do we stand? Where does the priest stand?

PROCESSIONAL/EXIT: What are we to do when we leave Mass during the week?

ACTIVITY #18

The Rosary Prayer Craft

The Rosary is one of the most beautiful prayers that we can pray alone or as a community. When praying the Rosary we learn about the life of Christ, as well as ourselves and our purpose in this world.

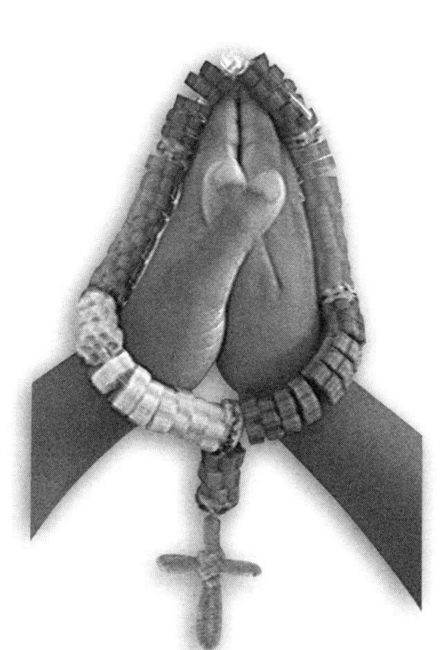

And he came to her and said, "Greetings, favored one! The Lord is with you."

(LUKE 1:28)

WHAT YOU NEED

- The Children's Rosary worksheet
- small threadable pasta (we used wagon wheel pasta) or six different colors of beads (red, blue, yellow, green, purple, and other)*
- food coloring (red, yellow, blue, and green)
- rubbing alcohol
- five plastic cups
- cookie sheet or aluminum foil
- paper towels
- string or yarn (two pieces per necklace; 8" and 32")
- tape (tape soft ends of yarn for easier threading)
- pipe cleaners (chenille stems), popsicle sticks, or anything that can be formed into a cross
- glue gun

***You'll need ten beads of red, blue, green, yellow, and purple, and four beads of "other" for each necklace. Fifty-four beads in total are needed.**

PREPARATION

1. Fill each plastic cup with 1⁄3 cup rubbing alcohol.
2. Pour one-half to three-quarters of each food coloring bottle into the plastic cups. To test the color, add a piece of pasta to each cup and let sit for five minutes. If the color is not bright enough, add more food coloring until the optimal color is achieved.
3. In the fifth plastic cup, pour the remaining red and some blue to obtain your fifth color, purple. Again, test the color by adding a piece of pasta and letting it sit for five minutes. Adjust the coloring as needed.
4. Set aside six uncolored pasta beads (per necklace). You will use these as your sixth color. To make the uncolored pasta more distinguishable from the yellow pasta, you can dot each piece with a black permanent marker.
5. Divide the remaining pasta into five equal parts. Place pasta into cups with dye solution.
6. Let pasta soak for five minutes and remove from cups.
7. While the pasta is soaking, place paper towels over aluminum foil.
8. Remove pasta from cups and place on paper towels. The pasta will be dry and ready to use in five minutes.
9. Make the tail of the rosary. Begin by making the cross. Bend and fold the chenille stem to form a cross.
10. Using the smaller string, thread one uncolored piece of pasta through the middle of the string.
11. Next, thread both ends of the string through one blue piece of pasta. Follow with a red, then green, and an uncolored piece of pasta. Finally, thread your cross through one end of the string, and tie both sides together to close off the tail of the rosary.

(*Note: If your cross does not have a loop to thread through, simply glue the cross to the last piece of uncolored pasta on the string.)

12. Assemble rosary kits.
    Each kit should include: one rosary tail, one 8" string, one 32" string, ten red pasta pieces, ten blue pasta pieces, ten green pasta pieces, ten yellow pasta pieces, ten purple pasta pieces, and four uncolored pasta pieces.
13. Review attached history of the Rosary for more learning tools about the Rosary.
14. Make copies of the Children's Rosary worksheet and Prayers of the Rosary to hand out to parents so they can pray with their child at home.

CRAFT TIME

1. Give each child a kit including "rosary kit" bag.
2. Have each child begin making the rosary by stringing one uncolored/other bead.
3. Next, add ten red beads.
4. Add another uncolored/other bead.
5. String ten blue beads.
6. Add the cross pendant, which will be the tail of the rosary.
7. Add ten yellow beads.
8. Add another uncolored/other bead.
9. Add ten green beads.
10. Add another uncolored/other bead.
11. Add ten purple beads.
12. Tie the rosary necklace together. Leave extra room so that the beads can move on the string. This will allow the children to grasp each individual bead as they count their prayers.
13. Pray!

A Brief History and Explanation of the Rosary

Tradition says that Saint Dominic designed the rosary. He received a vision from the Blessed Mother and she asked that we say prayers to help sinners get to heaven. The word "rosary" means wreath or crown of roses, and so when we say the Rosary, it is like offering spiritual roses to the mother of God. The rose is the queen of all flowers, just as the Blessed Mother is our Queen.

When we say the Rosary, we reflect on the life of Jesus Christ. We remember the stories of his life, or the mysteries of our Lord. These stories are called mysteries because every time we reflect upon them we learn more about the Lord, our world, and ourselves. Additionally, we refer to them as mysteries because we can never fully understand all there is to know about his life. This is why it is so important to continue to reflect and pray on these stories.

The mysteries are divided into four parts of Jesus' life. They are the joyous mysteries, the luminous mysteries, the sorrowful mysteries, and the glorious mysteries.

BE HAPPY

The joyous mysteries are just that! They are five stories about the birth and young life of Jesus Christ.

The first joyful mystery comes from Luke 1:26–38 and is called ***The Annunciation***. It is the story of the angel Gabriel coming to tell Mary that she would be the mother of Jesus Christ.

The second joyful mystery comes from Luke 1:39–56 and is called ***The Visitation***. This story tells of when Mary went to visit her cousin Elizabeth. She went to tell her how happy she was.

The third joyful mystery comes from Luke 2:1–20 and is called ***The Birth of Jesus***. This is the story of the (you guessed it!) birth of Jesus Christ.

The fourth joyful mystery comes from Luke 2:21–40 and is called ***The Presentation of the Child Jesus in the Temple***. This is when Mary and Joseph brought Jesus to the Temple to offer him to God.

The fifth joyful mystery comes from Luke 2:41–52 and is called ***The Finding of the Child Jesus in the Temple***. This is the story of Jesus getting lost and separated from his mother and father. They looked for him for three days, and found him in the Temple listening and talking about God.

THE LIGHT OF THE WORLD

The luminous mysteries are those stories that help us reflect on the love and the light Jesus brought to the world. They show us the good works that came from Jesus, and remind us to also help others in need.

The first luminous mystery comes from Mark 1:1–11, Mark 16:14, John 3:16, Acts 2:38, Galatians 3:27, and Romans 8:29–30 and is called ***The Baptism of Jesus in the Jordan River***.

The second luminous mystery comes from John 1:14, John 2:1–11, and Isaiah 62:4–5 and is called ***Miracle at the Cana Wedding Feast***. This is where Jesus turned water into wine.

The third luminous mystery comes from Mark 4:23, Luke 3:29, Mark 6:34, Mark 8:34, Luke 18:15–16, John 8:12, John 10:11, John 11:25, Luke 22:27, John 15:17 and is called ***Jesus Preaches Good News***. This is the story in which Jesus visits many places to teach about the love of God and to help and heal the poor and sick.

The fourth luminous mystery comes from Luke 9:28–36 and 1 John 3:1–2 and is called ***The Transfiguration***. In this story God shines a light all around

Jesus, and Jesus promises the disciples that they will also share in his light to the world.

The fifth luminous mystery comes from Matthew 26:20–22, 25–27, John 6:35, 54, John 14:3, John 14:27, John 15:12–13 and is called ***The Institution of the Eucharist***. This is the story in which Jesus first offered his Body and Blood to the disciples in the Last Supper.

THE SORROWFUL MYSTERIES

The sorrowful mysteries are the stories that recall when evil people decided to put Jesus to death. These are very sad stories that teach us that even in our hardest times God loves us and never leaves us.

The first sorrowful mystery comes from Mark 14:32–37, Luke 14:38, Mark 14:39, 41, 43, and 45 and is called ***The Agony of Jesus in the Garden***. This is where Jesus prayed because he was frightened for the pain that was to come. He prayed for God's help.

The second sorrowful mystery comes from John 18:28–30, 33, 36–37, 39–40 and John 19:1 and is called ***The Scourging at the Pillar***. This is where Jesus is beaten with whips.

The third sorrowful mystery comes from Mark 15:16, John 19:2–6, 8 and John 19:6 and is called ***The Crowning With Thorns***. This is where Jesus was made fun of and made to wear a crown of thorns.

The fourth sorrowful mystery comes from Matthew 26:56, Luke 23:26–28, 32–34, Luke 28:33–34, and Mark 15:23 and is called ***The Carrying of the Cross***.

The fifth sorrowful mystery comes from Mark 15, 26, 29, Luke 23:36, 46, John 19:25, Mark 15:33–34, 42–43, and 46–47 and is called the ***Crucifixion***. This is the sad story of when they nailed Jesus to the Cross and crucified him.

THE GLORY OF GOD

The glorious mysteries are the stories of Jesus after he died. They remind us of the everlasting life that God has promised us, and the Holy Spirit that he sent to help lead the way.

The first glorious mystery comes from John 20:1–2, 14–20 and is called ***The Resurrection of Jesus From the Dead***. This is the story of Jesus rising from the dead after being entombed for three days.

The second glorious mystery comes from Acts 1:1–4, 8–12, 14 and Mark 16:20 and is called ***The Ascension of Jesus Into Heaven***. This is when Jesus returned to heaven to be seated in his rightful place next to the Lord.

The third glorious mystery comes from John 14:16, John 15:26, Acts 2:1–5, 12, 14, and 16 and is called ***The Descent of the Holy Spirit***. This is when Jesus sent the Holy Spirit down from heaven to help lead our souls to heaven.

The fourth glorious mystery comes from Luke 1:46–47, 49–55 and is called ***The Assumption of Mary***. This story tells us that after Mary died, Jesus immediately pulled her up to heaven to be with him.

The fifth glorious mystery comes from Revelation 7:9, 12:1, 21:1–5, and 22:12 and is called ***Mary Crowned as Queen of the Angels and Saints***.

PRAYING THE ROSARY

When praying the Rosary, you get to decide which group of mysteries you want to pray. During Christmas you may want to remember the birth of Christ and pray the joyous mysteries; on Sundays you may want to remember the glory of the Lord and pray the glorious mysteries. Whatever your mood, you get to choose.

The Rosary is divided into five parts or decades. Each decade represents a particular mystery. As you start each new decade you should announce the mystery on which you will be reflecting. (See Rosary Key.) The beads are used as a reminder to tell you which prayer to say next. They also help you keep count, so that you're sure not to miss one!

The Rosary is a great prayer to say as a family. If you have young children, it may be advisable to do only one decade. Also, when teaching young children to say the Rosary, you may start out simple, by only saying the "Our Father" and the "Hail Mary" and when they are able, start adding additional prayers.

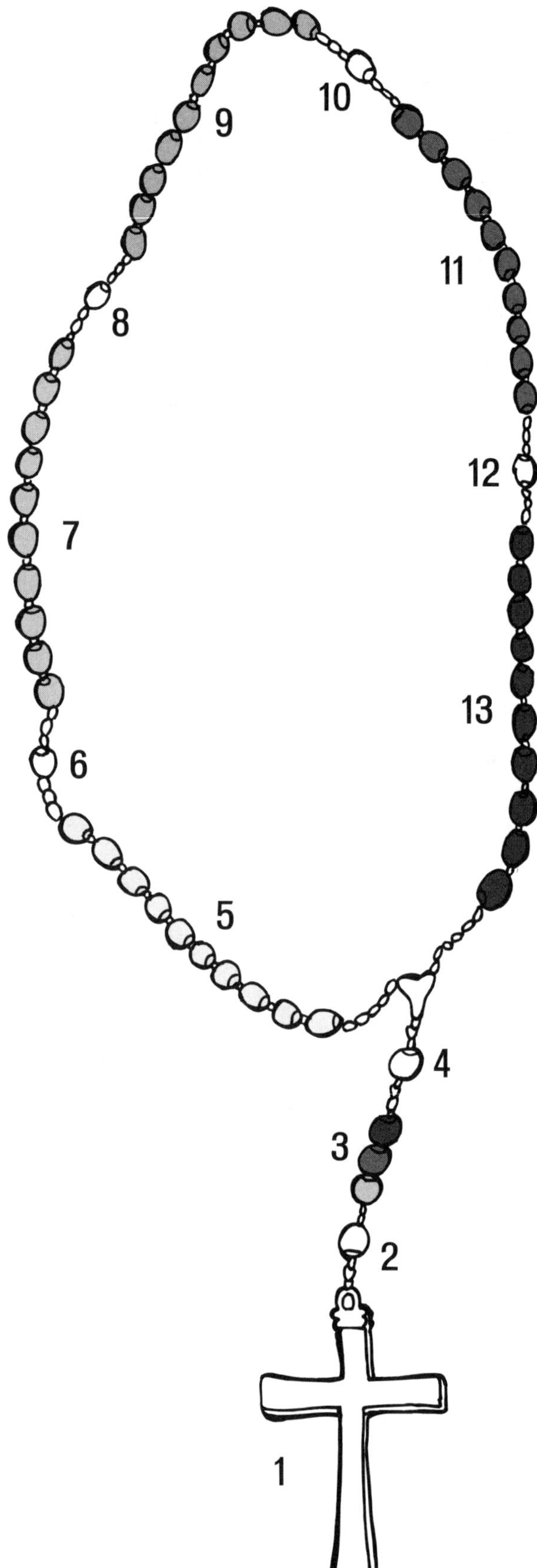

Rosary Key

1. Make the sign of the cross
   Say Apostles' Creed

2. Say Our Father

3. Say Hail Mary (3 total)
   Say Glory Be

4. Announce the mystery
   Say Our Father

5. Say one Hail Mary for each yellow bead
   (10 total)
   Say Glory Be*

6. Announce the mystery
   Say Our Father

7. Say one Hail Mary for each green bead
   (10 total)
   Say Glory Be*

8. Announce the mystery
   Say Our Father

9. Say one Hail Mary for each purple bead
   (10 total)
   Say Glory Be*

10. Announce the mystery
    Say Our Father

11. Say one Hail Mary for each red bead
    (10 total)
    Say Glory Be*

12. Announce the mystery
    Say Our Father

13. Say one Hail Mary for each blue bead
    (10 total)
    Say Glory Be*

End the Rosary by saying the Hail Holy Queen or a concluding prayer of your choice

**Optional: Pray O My Jesus. Some people say it after each decade (after the Glory Be). Some say it once at the end of the Rosary. And some do not say it at all.*

Prayers for the Rosary

THE APOSTLES CREED

I believe in God, the Father Almighty, Creator of heaven and Earth; and in Jesus Christ, his only Son, our Lord; who was conceived by the Holy Spirit, born of the Virgin Mary, suffered under Pontius Pilate, was crucified, died, and was buried. He descended into hell; the third day he arose again from the dead. He ascended into heaven, and sits at the right hand of God, the Father Almighty; from thence he shall come to judge the living and the dead. I believe in the Holy Spirit, the Holy Catholic Church, the communion of saints, the forgiveness of sins, the resurrection of the body, and life everlasting. Amen.

OUR FATHER

Our Father who art in heaven, hallowed be thy name; thy kingdom come; thy will be done on Earth as it is in heaven. Give us this day our daily bread; and forgive us our trespasses as we forgive those who trespass against us; and lead us not into temptation, but deliver us from evil. Amen.

HAIL MARY

Hail Mary, full of grace! The Lord is with thee; blessed are thou among women, and blessed is the fruit of thy womb, Jesus. Holy Mary, Mother of God, pray for us sinners now and at the hour of our death. Amen.

GLORY BE

Glory be to the Father, and to the Son, and to the Holy Spirit. As it was in the beginning, is now, and will be forever. Amen.

O MY JESUS

O my Jesus, forgive us our sins, save us from the fires of hell, and lead all souls to heaven, especially those in need of your mercy.

HAIL HOLY QUEEN

Hail, holy Queen, Mother of mercy, hail, our life, our sweetness, and our hope. To thee do we cry, poor banished children of Eve. To thee do we send up our sighs, mourning and weeping in this valley of tears. Turn then, most gracious advocate, thine eyes of mercy toward us. And after this our exile, show unto us the blessed Fruit of thy womb, Jesus. O clement, O loving, O sweet Virgin Mary!

Pray for us, O holy Mother of God. That we may be made worthy of the promises of Christ.

Let us pray: O God, whose only-begotten Son, by his life, death, and resurrection, has purchased for us the rewards of eternal life, grant, we beseech You, that meditating upon these mysteries of the Holy Rosary of the Blessed Virgin Mary, we may imitate what they contain and obtain what they promise, through the same Christ, our Lord. Amen.

Holy Spirit Windsock Craft

What if you had someone help you with everything you do, all the time? What if that person never left, was always in your heart, in your mind, and in the air you breathe? Well, we all have that special someone called the Holy Spirit. The Bible tells us that when Jesus went to live with God in heaven, he sent the Holy Spirit down to help and guide us to be good people.

When we read about the Holy Spirit in the Bible, we learn that God sent down the Holy Spirit in the form of a dove. A dove, which is graceful and gentle, was sent to us to help our hearts soar. In this craft we remember the presence of the Holy Spirit in our hearts and in the air all around. Let's decorate a windsock with flying doves to remind us to fly high in the Spirit!

And I will ask the Father, and he will give you another Advocate, to be with you for ever.

(JOHN 14:16)

WHAT YOU NEED

Dove and Windsock Cutouts worksheets

8" x 11" colored paper

pen or pencil

hole punch

string or yarn (three 12"-long pieces per child)

streamers (five 24"-long strips per child)

glue stick

tape or stapler

PREPARATION

1. Draw five Xs at the bottom of your colored paper as indicated below.

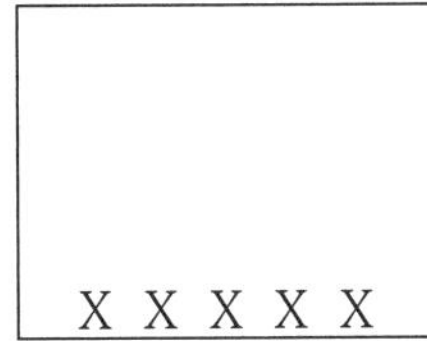

2. Punch three holes at the top of your colored paper approximately 2½" apart.
3. Tie each one of the three strings to the three holes at the top of your paper. Secure the loose ends of the string by tying one knot (near the top), being careful not to tear your paper.

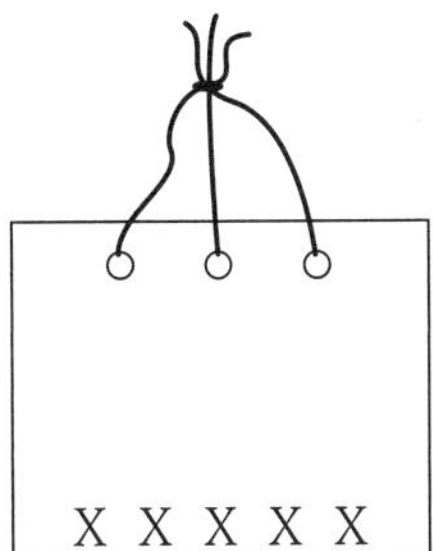

4. Copy and cut out the doves from the handout.
5. Cut five streamers per child.
6. Copy and cut out the words "Holy Spirit" from the handout. The word "Holy" will fit on one streamer and the word "Spirit" will fit on another. Each child should have one "Holy" and one "Spirit."
7. Copy the Bible verses onto colored paper. Cut out each verse (two per child).
8. Assemble kits.

   Each kit should include: one colored paper with Xs and string, three doves, five streamers, one Holy cutout, one Spirit cutout, and two Bible verses. Each kit can be paper-clipped together for easy distribution.

CRAFT TIME

1. Hand out a kit to each child.
2. Rub the glue stick over the five Xs on the colored paper.
3. Glue the end of each streamer to one of the Xs at the bottom of the paper. Turn the paper over to the clean side.
4. Put glue on the back of the cutouts "HOLY" and "SPIRIT."
5. Place each cutout vertically on separate streamers. (The order doesn't matter because the finished craft is cylindrical.)
6. Fold the wings of the dove cutouts upward along the dotted lines.
7. Put glue on the back of the dove cutouts, making sure not to put glue on the wings. Place the doves on the colored paper. Open their wings.
8. Put glue on the back of the Scripture cutouts.
9. Place Scripture cutouts on the colored paper.
10. Finally, tape the ends of the colored paper to make a cylindrical windsock. Be sure to securely tape or staple the top, bottom, and middle for a sturdy "sock." Go outside and enjoy watching the windsocks blow in the wind!

Dove Cutouts

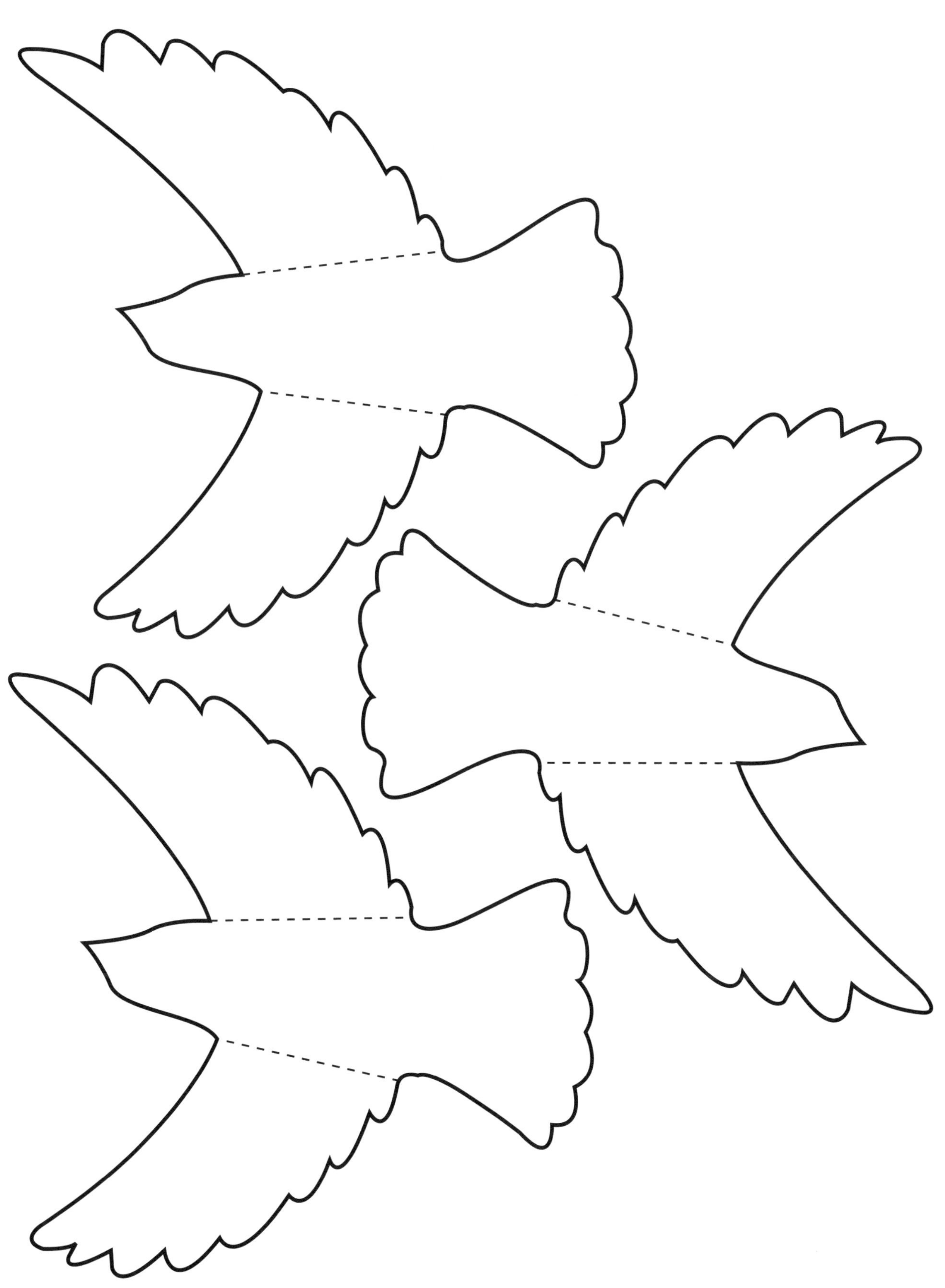

Windsock Cutouts

H
O
L
Y

S
P
I
R
I
T

"I will ask the Father, and he will give you another Advocate, to be with you forever." JOHN 14:16

"...and the Holy Spirit descended upon him in bodily form like a dove. And a voice came from heaven. 'You are my son, the beloved; with you I am well pleased.'" LUKE 3:21-22

"I Make Choices" Memory Tree

Every day we are given the opportunity to make choices and decisions. We always want to try to make good choices, even when we are tempted to make a bad choice. We must ask the Holy Spirit to guide us in our daily activities and lead us in the direction that is good.

Today we are going to make a fruit tree, similar to the one that was in the Garden of Eden. Our tree will have both tasty sweet fruit and sour bitter fruit. Which fruit will you choose? The choice may not be as easy as it seems!

**Note: A helpful Bible story that goes well with this activity is the story of Adam and Eve being banished from the Garden of Eden. You may want to read this story aloud in class and discuss with the children temptations that we all face in our lives. It is important to reiterate the fact that when we have a difficult choice to make, we always have help through the Holy Spirit and our families.*

Choose what is good.

(BASED ON ISAIAH 7:15)

WHAT YOU NEED

Game Instructions, Tree Outline, Apple Shapes, Trunk Outline, and Choices Cutouts worksheets
green paper (one per child)
brown paper (one for every three children)
red paper (one per child)
white paper (two per child)
scissors and/or exacto knife
glue stick

PREPARATION

1. Review Game Instructions worksheet.
2. Print or copy the Tree Outline on the green paper. Cut out the tree. On each dotted line on the tree, cut a slit with your scissors or exacto knife.
3. Next, print or copy the Trunk Outline onto the brown paper. Cut out the tree trunks.
4. Using the red paper, print or copy the Apple Shapes. Cut out each apple. Each child should have eight apples for his or her tree.
5. Copy the Choices Cutouts worksheet onto the other sheet of white paper. Cut out each individual picture.
6. Copy the Game Instructions onto the back side of the white paper. This will help the parents understand the object of the game when the children go home.
7. Assemble kits.
   Each kit should include: eight apples, eight "choices" pictures, one tree outline, one trunk outline, and one instruction sheet.

CRAFT TIME

1. Give each child a craft kit.
2. On the plain side of the instruction sheet, glue the trunk of the tree so that approximately seven-eighths of the trunk is OFF the page.
3. Next, carefully glue along the edges of the tree outline. Only a little is needed, because too much will interfere with the apples sliding into the "pockets" on the tree.
4. Glue each "choices" picture onto the back side of an apple. Each child should have eight apples, each with a different picture.
5. Slide each apple into a different pocket on the tree.
6. Play the game!

Game Instructions

This game is based on the Sunday school lesson "We Make Choices." It is intended to show your child that they make choices and decisions every day. We always want to make good choices, even when we are tempted to make bad ones. We ask the Holy Spirit to guide us in our daily activities and lead us in the direction that is good.

To play: Each child has eight apples that fit into the pockets on the tree. On the back of each apple, the child is presented with either a good choice or a bad choice.

Tell the child to pick one apple. Once they identify what "choice" is on the back, they must then find its opposite. As in the game Memory, when they pull an apple, if the apple is not the opposing "choice" then they should return both apples to the tree. They should continue pulling until they find all four pairs. The pairs are indicated below.

Good Choice	Bad Choice
Eat fruit	Eat candy
Be happy	Be mad or sad
Help clean	Make a mess
Do homework	Watch TV

Have fun!

NOTE: ***While the choices in this game are simple, we know that everything in God's kingdom has its place, and that real-life choices are not always so black and white. However, these examples are used only to represent different types of behavior on a basic level. Further discussion may be needed to allow the children to discuss situations in which all of these behaviors could be viewed as acceptable, and other situations in which they would not be appropriate.***

Tree Outline

Trunk Outline

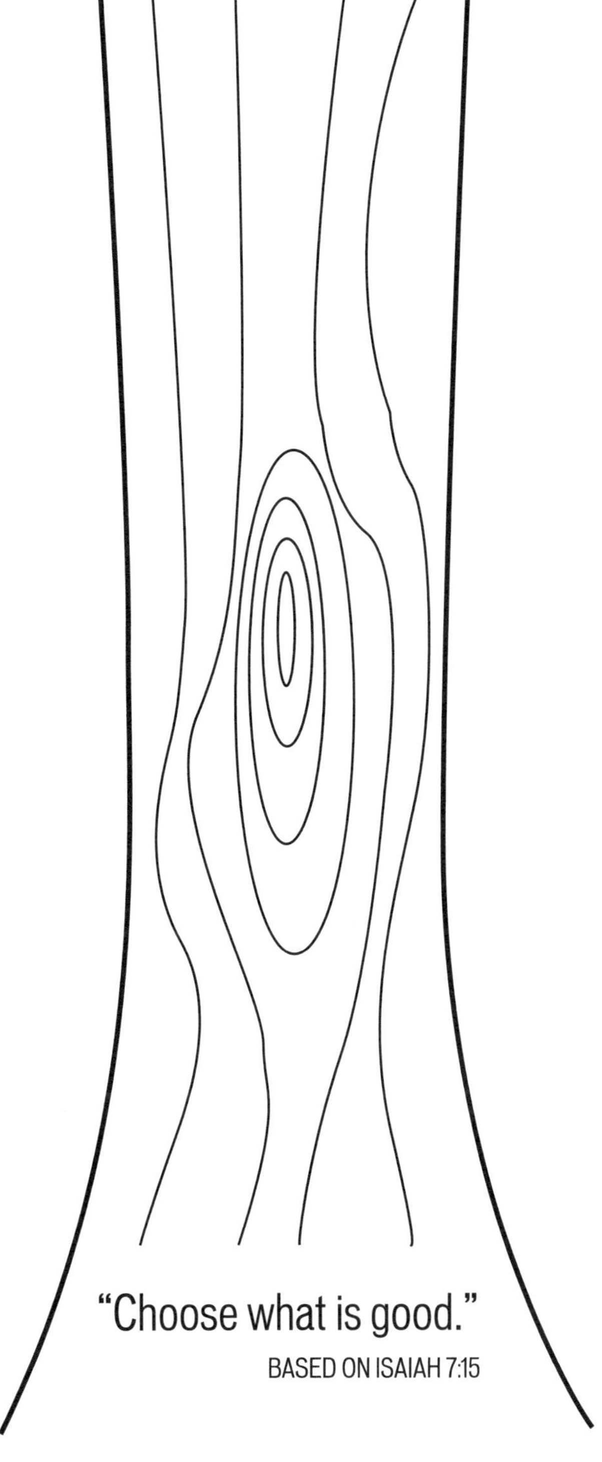

Apple Shapes

Choices Cutouts

Eat candy

Eat fruit

Help clean

Make a mess

Be happy

Be mad or sad

Do homework

Watch TV

ACTIVITY #21

Love Him and Praise Him–Tambourine Craft

How many ways can we show God that we love him? We can talk to him in prayer, we can be kind to those around us, and we can volunteer to help those who need our help. Another way to show God that we love him is to proclaim his word for all to hear. We can sing and dance in the name of the Lord. Do you like to sing and dance and tell about the Lord's goodness? Then you'll love this craft where we make tambourines to play loudly while singing to the Lord's good news!

Praise him with tambourine and dance; praise him with strings and pipe! Let everything that breathes praise the Lord! Praise the Lord!

(PSALMS 150:4,6)

WHAT YOU NEED

Praise Him Verse worksheet

small styrofoam or paper plate

tissue paper of various colors and patterns

string

glue stick

large jingle bells (three per tambourine)

plain 8" x 10" typing paper

PREPARATION

1. Poke three separate holes in three opposite edges of the plate.
2. Cut tissue paper into 2" x 2" pieces.
3. Cut three pieces of yarn per tambourine approximately 8" long.
4. Copy or print Praise Him Bible Verse worksheet onto plain white paper. Cut out one verse per tambourine.
5. Assemble kits.
   Each kit should include: one paper plate with three holes, three pieces of yarn, three jingle bells, and one Bible verse.

CRAFT TIME

1. Hand out pre-assembled kits.
2. Thread a piece of yarn through one of the holes in the paper plate. Next, thread a jingle bell through the yarn and tie to secure. Repeat this process until all three jingle bells are tied to the plate.
3. Glue the tissue paper all over the plate, until no white is showing.
4. Glue the Praise Him Bible Verse in the center of the plate.
5. Turn on a Bible songs tape or CD and have the children sing along while playing their tambourines!

Praise Him Bible Verse

Praise him with tambourine and dance;
praise him with strings...!
Let everything that breathes praise the Lord!
Praise the Lord!
PSALM 150:4, 6

Praise him with tambourine and dance;
praise him with strings...!
Let everything that breathes praise the Lord!
Praise the Lord!
PSALM 150:4, 6

Praise him with tambourine and dance;
praise him with strings...!
Let everything that breathes praise the Lord!
Praise the Lord!
PSALM 150:4, 6

Praise him with tambourine and dance;
praise him with strings...!
Let everything that breathes praise the Lord!
Praise the Lord!
PSALM 150:4, 6

Praise him with tambourine and dance;
praise him with strings...!
Let everything that breathes praise the Lord!
Praise the Lord!
PSALM 150:4, 6

Praise him with tambourine and dance;
praise him with strings...!
Let everything that breathes praise the Lord!
Praise the Lord!
PSALM 150:4, 6

Praise him with tambourine and dance;
praise him with strings...!
Let everything that breathes praise the Lord!
Praise the Lord!
PSALM 150:4, 6

Praise him with tambourine and dance;
praise him with strings...!
Let everything that breathes praise the Lord!
Praise the Lord!
PSALM 150:4, 6

Praise him with tambourine and dance;
praise him with strings...!
Let everything that breathes praise the Lord!
Praise the Lord!
PSALM 150:4, 6

Praise him with tambourine and dance;
praise him with strings...!
Let everything that breathes praise the Lord!
Praise the Lord!
PSALM 150:4, 6

Praise him with tambourine and dance;
praise him with strings...!
Let everything that breathes praise the Lord!
Praise the Lord!
PSALM 150:4, 6

Praise him with tambourine and dance;
praise him with strings...!
Let everything that breathes praise the Lord!
Praise the Lord!
PSALM 150:4, 6

Praise him with tambourine and dance;
praise him with strings...!
Let everything that breathes praise the Lord!
Praise the Lord!
PSALM 150:4, 6

Praise him with tambourine and dance;
praise him with strings...!
Let everything that breathes praise the Lord!
Praise the Lord!
PSALM 150:4, 6

Praise him with tambourine and dance;
praise him with strings...!
Let everything that breathes praise the Lord!
Praise the Lord!
PSALM 150:4, 6

Praise him with tambourine and dance;
praise him with strings...!
Let everything that breathes praise the Lord!
Praise the Lord!
PSALM 150:4, 6

Praise him with tambourine and dance;
praise him with strings...!
Let everything that breathes praise the Lord!
Praise the Lord!
PSALM 150:4, 6

Praise him with tambourine and dance;
praise him with strings...!
Let everything that breathes praise the Lord!
Praise the Lord!
PSALM 150:4, 6

Praise him with tambourine and dance;
praise him with strings...!
Let everything that breathes praise the Lord!
Praise the Lord!
PSALM 150:4, 6

Praise him with tambourine and dance;
praise him with strings...!
Let everything that breathes praise the Lord!
Praise the Lord!
PSALM 150:4, 6

Praise him with tambourine and dance;
praise him with strings...!
Let everything that breathes praise the Lord!
Praise the Lord!
PSALM 150:4, 6

ACTIVITY #22

Be Kind Sunflower Craft

One of the most important lessons we can learn is to be kind. Jesus tells us the story of the good neighbor (Luke 10:29–37) in which we see the importance of loving our neighbors, no matter what our differences. It isn't always easy to be helpful, kind, or nice to our neighbors. But if we ask for Jesus' help, we can find the strength to love and help others just as he did. You too can be a good neighbor by helping around the house, taking care of a sick friend or pet, or just by being nice to your brother or sister. There are many ways to show your kindness. Today, let's show our kindness by making a beautiful sunflower and giving it to someone we love!

Be kind to one another.

(EPHESIANS 4:32)

WHAT YOU NEED

Sunflower worksheet with poem
Petals, Flower Center, Flower Stem worksheets
Leaves worksheet or real leaves
colored paper for copies (assorted yellows for petals, brown or tan for flower center, and green for the flower stem and leaves)
scissors
glue sticks
glitter (*optional*)

PREPARATION

1. Make one copy of the Sunflower worksheet for each child (pastel colored paper works well with this project).
2. Make colored copies of the Petal, Flower Center, Flower Stem, and Leaves worksheets. Cut out each figure on the various worksheets. Each child will need thirteen petals, one flower center, one flower stem, and two leaves.
3. Assemble kits. Each kit should include: one Sunflower worksheet, thirteen petals, one flower center, one flower stem, and two leaves.

CRAFT TIME

1. Give each child a pre-assembled kit.
2. Glue the stem on first. ***(*Note: The stem is long, so it may hang off the page. It is okay if it overlaps onto the flower center, as it will be covered later.)***
3. Glue on the two leaves.
4. Glue on each of the thirteen petals.
5. Glue on the flower center.
6. Rub glue on the top of the flower center once it is affixed. Sprinkle with glitter. Now you have a beautiful gift to help you share your kind heart!

Sunflower

"Be kind to one another."

EPHESIANS 4:32

Jesus said to be kind,
and I've got you in mind.
Here's a flower to let you know
how we both love you so!

Petals

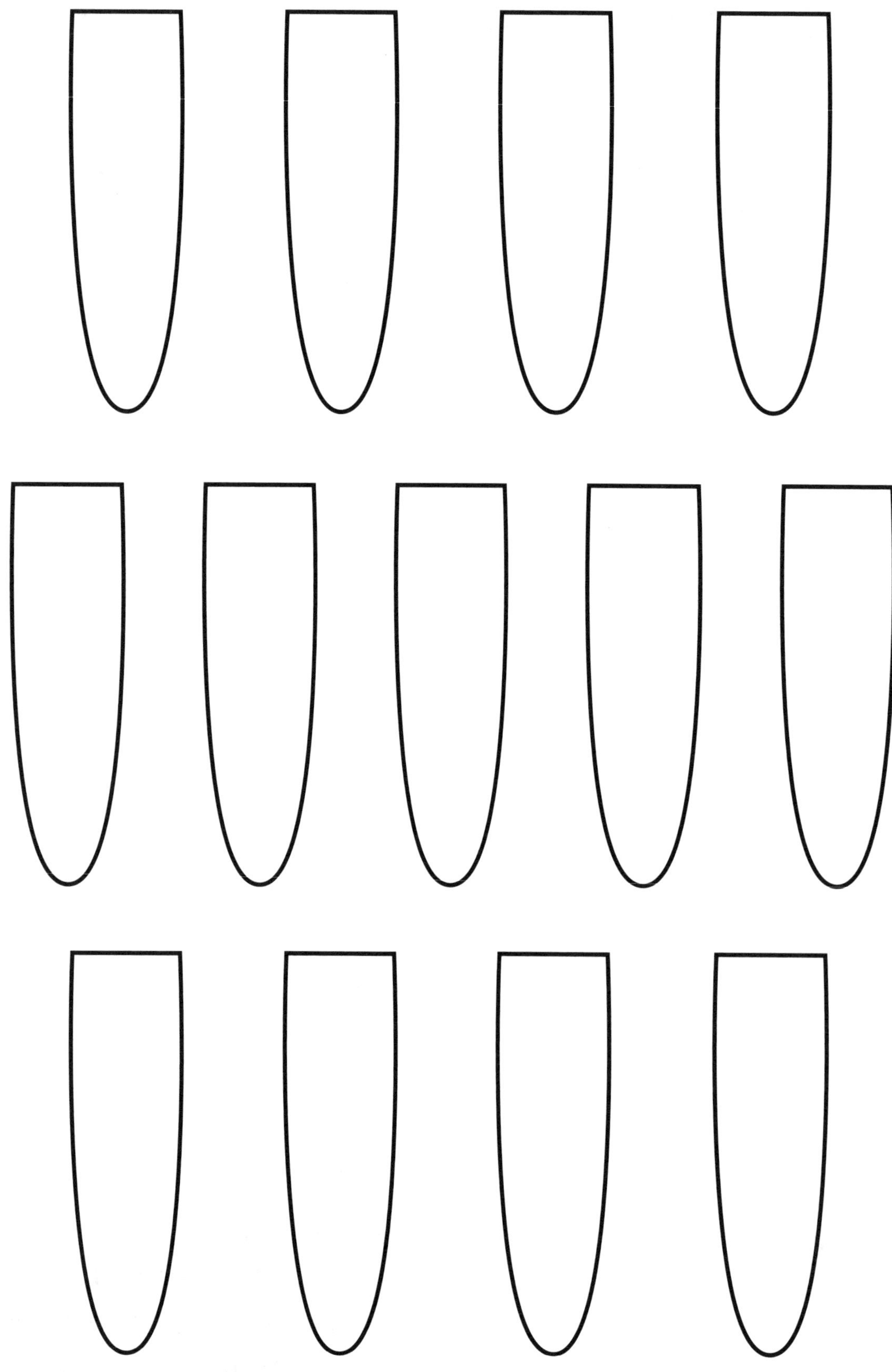

Flower Center / Stem / Leaves

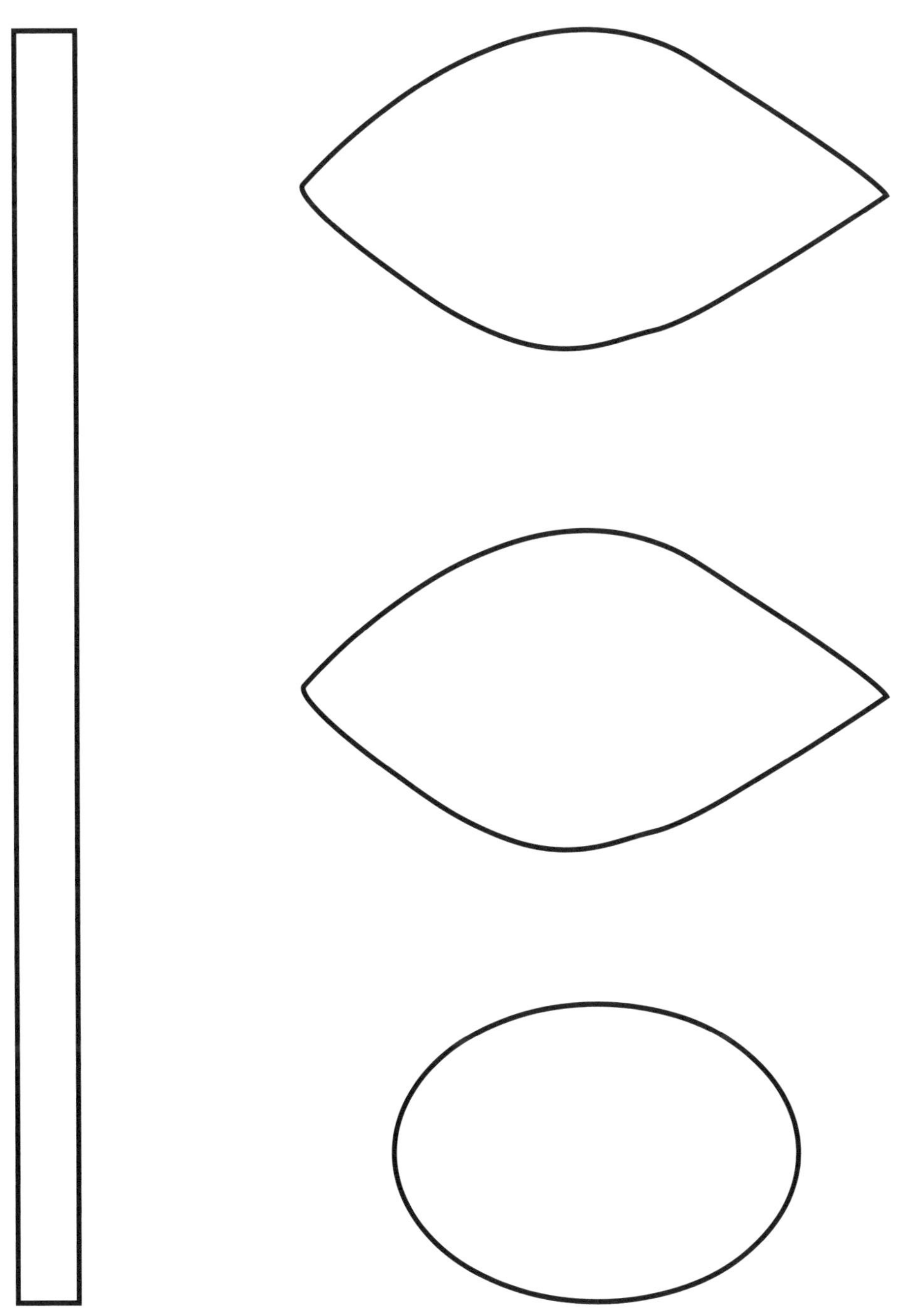

ACTIVITY #23

We Take Care of Ourselves Fruit Pizza Project

God loved each of us so much that he gave us the gift of life. With the life that God gives us we can be kind, love others, and help take care of those in need. We can each show God how thankful we are by also loving ourselves. How do we do that? We love ourselves by laughing, playing, exercising, taking care of ourselves, and eating good things that make our minds and bodies strong. All of these things are important because that is how we show others the glory of the Lord. So, let's show God we love him by making a healthy and delicious fruit pizza that will give us plenty of energy to love, work, and play!

He satisfies you with good as long as you live so that your youth is renewed like the eagles.

(PSALMS 103:5)

WHAT YOU NEED

We Take Care of Ourselves Fruit Pizza Recipe handout (one copy per child)

paper plates

napkins

plastic knives or craft sticks

Fruit Pizza Recipe (on handout)

large whole wheat refrigerated biscuits

8-ounce package of low-fat cream cheese

½ cup sugar (*optional*)

assorted fruit (canned pineapple, mandarins, peaches, fruit cocktail, or fresh fruit including bananas, strawberries, kiwi, blueberries, etc.)

PREPARATION

1. Bake biscuits according to package instructions. Let cool.
2. While the biscuits are baking, cream together the sugar and cream cheese. Place cream cheese sauce into a plastic container and place in refrigerator until ready to use.
3. Split each biscuit into equal halves to create mini pizza rounds.
4. Gather, cut, and/or drain assorted fruit. Place fruit in plastic container and refrigerate until ready to use.
5. Assemble kits.

   Each kit should include: one paper plate, one napkin, one plastic knife/craft stick, and one Fruit Pizza Recipe (to share with their family).

PROJECT TIME

1. Hand out pre-assembled kits.
2. Give each child one pizza round and four to five pieces of fruit.
3. Place one teaspoon of cream cheese sauce on each child's plate.
4. Have the children gently spread the cream cheese sauce all over the pizza round with their utensils.
5. Next, they can top the pizza with their favorite fruit toppings.
6. Finally, eat and enjoy!

We Take Care of Ourselves

Fruit Pizza Recipe

Dear Family,

Today in class we learned all about taking care of ourselves. We learned that God loved each of us so much that he gave us the gift of life. With the life that God gives us we can be kind, love others, and help take care of those in need. We can each show God how thankful we are by also loving ourselves. How do we do that? We love ourselves by laughing, playing, exercising, taking care of ourselves, and eating good things that make our minds and bodies strong. All of these things are important because that is how we show others the glory of the Lord. Today we showed God we love him by making a healthy and delicious fruit pizza that will give us plenty of energy to love, work, and play!

Try this fun and healthy recipe at home! Every time you take a bite out of this scrumptious pizza, remember that you are taking care of yourself by eating a healthy and nutritious snack that you made yourself. God gave you the gift of life, and we rejoice in him every time we do something good for ourselves. So, eat up and have fun!

INGREDIENTS

large whole wheat refrigerated biscuits*

8-ounce package of cream cheese

½ cup sugar (*optional*)

assorted fruit (canned pineapple, mandarins, peaches, fruit cocktail, or fresh fruit including bananas, strawberries, kiwi, blueberries, etc.)

DIRECTIONS

1. Bake biscuits as directed. Let cool.
2. Cream together the sugar and cream cheese. Set aside.
3. Split each biscuit into two equal parts to create pizza rounds.
4. Spread with one tablespoon of cream cheese sauce.
5. Top pizza with favorite fruit toppings.
6. Enjoy!

Note: Also try using whole wheat English muffins, bagels, or refrigerated pizza dough cut into squares as another easy alternative.

The Prodigal Piggy Craft

Have you ever had to say "I'm sorry"? At one time or another, all people have to say these very same words. Jesus once told a story about saying sorry and about forgiveness. This story is in the book of Luke 15:11–24. The story is about a father and his two sons, and how the power of saying "I'm sorry" can turn a sad man into a happy man.

WHAT YOU NEED

- The Prodigal Son Book worksheets
- Piggy Face, Mouth, and Nose Cutout worksheets
- white 8" x 10" typing paper (four sheets per book plus more for pig face cutouts)
- pink or peach typing paper
- stapler
- marshmallows
- wiggly craft eyes

There was a rich man who had two sons. One day the younger son said, "Father, give me my half of the property now." So the father divided the property between the two sons. Within a few days the younger son sold his property and left town with all the money.

The younger son went to a country far away, and he spent all his money on reckless and wild living. Soon a famine came over the land, and he had to work for a man who offered him a job taking care of and feeding dirty pigs. Even the pigs lived better than he did, for they had bean pods to eat, yet he could not get anything to eat. "How did this happen to me? My father's workers have plenty of food to eat, and I am starving to death! I will go ask my father to please forgive me and allow me to work as one of his hired men, as I am not worthy to be called his son." So he went to his father.

When his father saw the younger son coming down the road, he ran to him! The son said, "Father, I have sinned against you. I am not worthy to be called your son."

But the father said, "Son, I am so happy that you are here!" The father called to his servants, "Bring the best robe for my son! We shall kill a prize calf for a feast! For my son was dead, and now he is alive; he was lost, but now he has been found." And so the feasting began.

(BASED ON LUKE 15:11–24)

PREPARATION

1. Copy or print The Prodigal Son Book worksheets onto white paper. Cut out along dotted lines. Place each sheet of the booklet in numerical order, with the title page on the top. Paper clip to secure.
2. The Piggy Face worksheet and the Piggy Nose worksheet should be printed on pink/peach paper. The Piggy Mouth worksheet should be printed on white paper. Cut out two piggy heads, one piggy nose, and one piggy mouth for each child.
3. Assemble the kits. Each kit should include: two piggy heads, one Prodigal Piggy Booklet paper-clipped together, one piggy nose, one piggy mouth, five marshmallows, and two wiggly eyes.

CRAFT TIME

1. Hand out the pre-assembled kits.
2. Glue the eyes, nose, and mouth onto one of the piggy faces.
3. Lick one end of each marshmallow and stick them in the mouth of the pig. These are the pig's teeth! Make sure you lick them good so they'll stay on. Some marshmallows may come up missing, so you may want to have extra, just in case!
4. Make a booklet by sandwiching the pre-cut story pages between the piggy marshmallow face (cover) and the other piggy head. Staple to secure.
5. Have fun sharing the story with a friend!

Piggy heads / Snout / Mouth

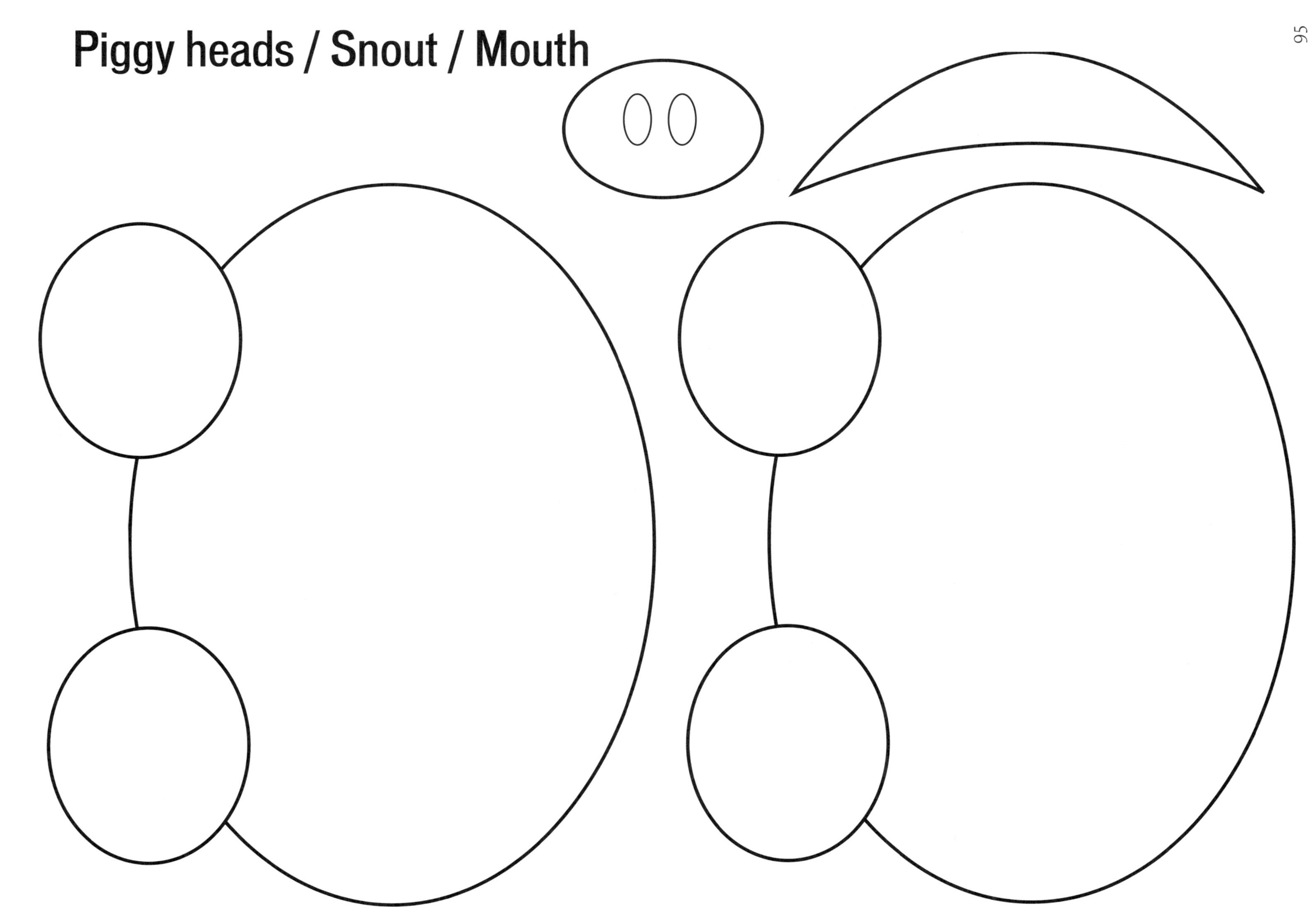

Piggy Story 1

THE PRODIGAL SON

A story Jesus told about
saying "Sorry" and forgiveness

BASED ON LUKE 15:11-32

1

There was once a very rich man
who had two mature sons.
The older was a helping hand.
The younger just wanted to have fun.
The younger son went to the father,
proclaiming all the way,
"I want my half of the property,
and I would like it today!"
The father, not knowing what to think,
divided his property in half.
Half went to the older son,
and half went to the younger man.

2

What do you think they did with the land?
Work on it and labor all day?
While your answer is partially right,
there is much more left to say.

The older brother, a good son he was,
continued to work and do what was right.
But the younger brother, so foolish he was,
sold his property that very night.

You see, all he wanted was the money,
to spend and use as he wished.
So he packed up his belongings
and moved away, without even a kiss.

3

He went to a country far away,
and there he spent all his cash.
He used it up on reckless living;
he spent everything that he had.

Soon the skies turned very dark,
and famine came over the land.
People were starving, with no food or drink,
and he too had nothing in his hands.

He met a man who offered him work,
a job working on a farm.
Feeding the pigs, cleaning their filth,
and keeping them from harm.

4

Now this was a job that no one wanted–
taking care of dirty pigs–
but these pigs had slop and bean pods to eat,
whereas the son had not even a twig.

The life of a pig was better than his,
for hunger pains was all he could feel,
"I'm starving to death," he bemoaned and groaned,
but no one brought him a meal.

He finally came to his senses when he thought,
"Why do I stay here and starve all day?
My father's workers have more than they can eat,
and I stay here and work like a slave.

Piggy Story 2

5

"I'll tell my father, 'I'm sorry,'
and that I'm not fit to be his son.
For I have sinned against God and him,
so only as a worker do I come."

So he began his long journey home
and when he had not yet arrived,
his father saw him in the distance
and ran toward his son and cried.

The father opened his arms very wide
and wrapped his arms around him.
He gave his son a gentle kiss
and, with a pitying heart, forgave his sins.

6

"Father," cried out the foolish son,
"I have sinned against God and you–
I am not fit to be called your son.
For this I know to be true!"

But the father called to his servants,
"Put a ring on his finger and shoes on his feet.
He shall have the finest robe
and a prize calf for a feast!"

And so these gifts were brought to his son,
and the feast and celebration began
"This son of mine was lost and dead
and now is alive and at hand."

7

The older son was in the field
when he heard the dancing and music.
He called over to one of the servants
and inquired about all the chanting.

"Your younger brother has come home,"
the servant quickly replied.
"Your father has killed his most prized calf
because he returned," he sighed.

The older brother became furious,
and the house he would not go in.
The father begged him to come join the fun,
but his son refused him again.

8

"I have worked like a slave for many years,"
ranted the older of the sons.
"I have never disobeyed your orders,
and from you what have I won?
"Not even a goat to eat with my friends!
Oh, you've made a grave mistake!
He has wasted away all your money,
and you kill a prize calf for his sake."
"My son, you are always here with me,
and everything that I have is yours.
Let us be happy and celebrate–
that is what a family is for.

9

"Your brother was lost and now is found.
He was dead and now he lives.
He lives because he was sorry
and because of our power to forgive."

ACTIVITY #25

Prayer Cross Craft

Every prayer that we say can be as beautiful and lovely as our most cherished poem or story. It's nice to have a beautiful reminder to pray, something that physically shows our love for God as we spiritually grow in him.

We see Mommy and Daddy every day, so we don't have to remember to talk to them. But God is our Father also, and sometimes we forget that he is with us all the time. Whenever we want, we can talk to God. We can always tell him good or bad things, and he will always listen. Let's make a cross as a symbol and a reminder of our love and our willingness to pray.

Whatever you ask for
in prayer with faith,
you will receive.

(MATTHEW 21:22)

WHAT YOU NEED

Prayer Cross Outline and Prayer Scripture and Contact Paper Cross Outline worksheets

dried wildflowers and/or leaves (see Two-Minute Quick-Dry Instructions on page 100)

white construction paper or hard stock paper

scissors

hole punch

yarn

tape

glue stick

clear contact paper

manila folders (*for assembling kits, optional*)

PREPARATION

1. If you don't already have dried flowers and/or leaves, follow the Quick-Dry Instructions on page 100 to learn how to dry your own.
2. Gather the dried wildflowers and/or leaves. Since the size of each flower may vary, determine how many each child will need for their Prayer Cross. Set aside.
3. Make one copy per child of the Prayer Cross Outline and Prayer Scripture worksheet onto white construction or hard stock paper.
4. Next, punch twenty-eight holes around the perimeter of each cross (designated by the Xs).
5. Cut one piece of yarn per cross approximately 60" long.
6. Tightly wrap tape around one end of the yarn several times. This will help the children thread the yarn around the cross easier.
7. Tape the other end of the yarn (the end without the tape) to the upper back of the cross.
8. Cut out the Contact Paper Outline Cross from the worksheet. Use this as an outline to trace the form onto the contact paper. Cut out each cross outline from the contact paper. You need one contact paper cross per construction paper cross.
9. Assemble kits in folders. First place the dried flowers and one Scripture verse for each child between paper towels or napkins. (This helps to protect the delicate flowers and stops them from slipping.) Place them in the folder along with construction paper cross.
10. Set aside the contact paper crosses (these are not to be handed out to the children).

2-MINUTE QUICK-DRY INSTRUCTIONS FOR DRYING AND PRESSING WILDFLOWERS AND LEAVES

1. Gather the flowers and leaves you would like to dry.
2. Remove any part of the plant that you do not want to press and dry.
3. Place one paper towel in the microwave.
4. Lay your flowers and/or leaves on top of the paper towel.
5. Place another paper towel on top the flowers and/or leaves.
6. Place a large heavy object (i.e., heavy plate, casserole dish) over the top and firmly press down.
7. Microwave your flowers and leaves for approximately two minutes. Each microwave varies, so your time might be slightly longer or shorter.
8. Remove the dried materials from the microwave and pull away from the paper towel. You have a dried and pressed flower in two minutes!

If for some reason the flower sticks to the paper towel, place them in the freezer until cold and slowly remove the flower. The flowers should release much easier.

CRAFT TIME

1. Hand out the pre-assembled kits.
2. Glue the Scripture verse onto the side of the cross that does not have yarn taped to it.
3. Glue the dried flowers and leaves on the cross.
4. Remove the backing from the contact paper cross and place in the center of the decorated cross. Press firmly and smooth to eliminate any air bubbles.
5. Begin threading the yarn around the perimeter of the cross by pulling it in and out of the holes around the cross.
6. End by tying a knot and making a hanger with the excess yarn at the top of the cross. Hang and enjoy!

Prayer Cross Outline and Prayer Scripture

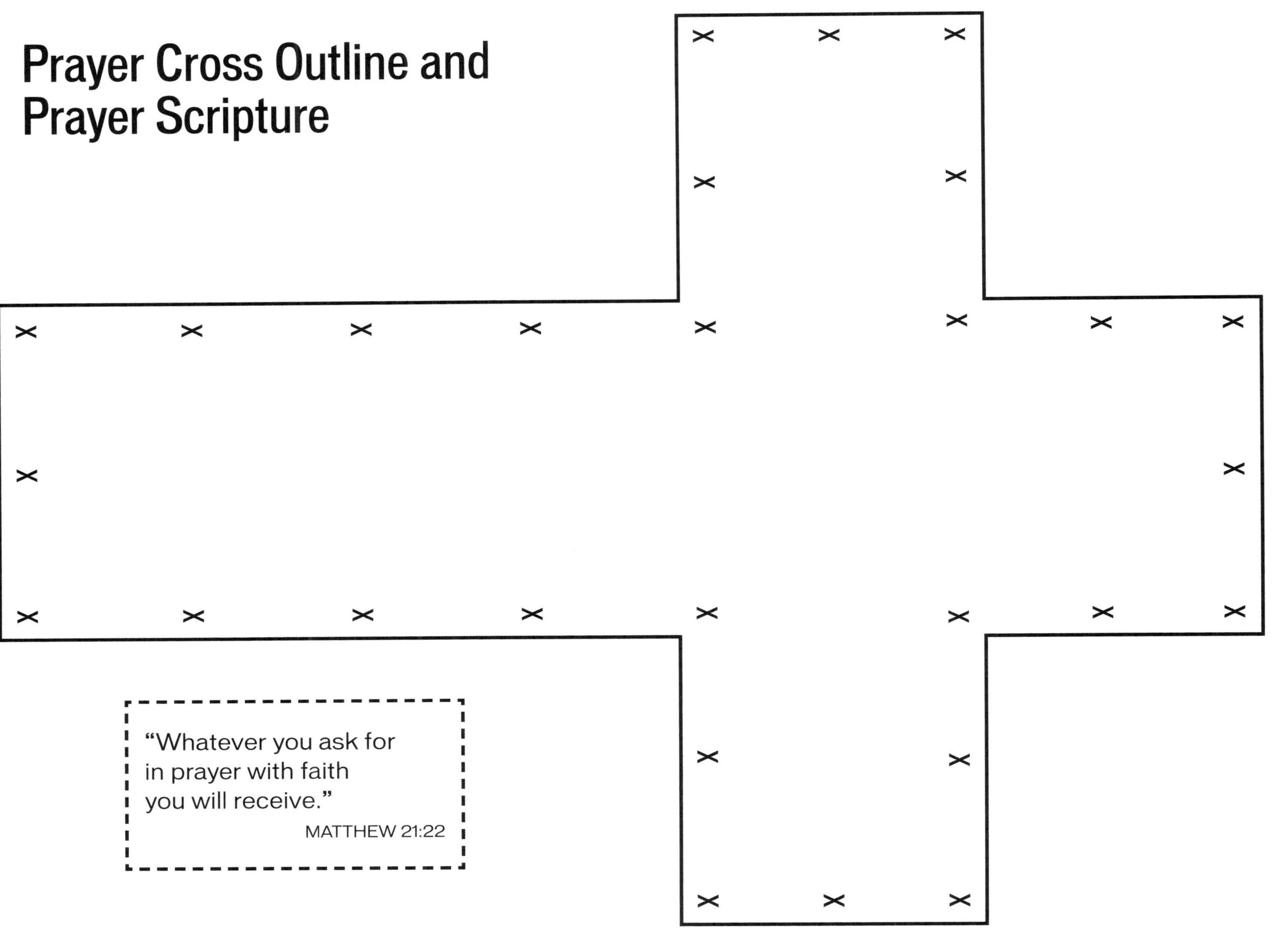

"Whatever you ask for
in prayer with faith
you will receive."
MATTHEW 21:22

Contact Paper Cross Outline

ACTIVITY #26

Happy Birthday Mary Craft

Did you know that everybody has a birthday? How do you and your family celebrate birthdays? Do you buy presents or have cake and ice cream? Well, the church celebrates birthdays, too. One of the most important birthdays that the church celebrates is the Virgin Mary's. Mary was the mother of Jesus and is a very special person in the church. Every year, during the Feast of the Birth of the Virgin Mary on September 8, the church celebrates this very special day. Today, let's celebrate Mary's birthday by making her a birthday cake to say "We love you!"

Blessed are you among women, and blessed is the fruit of your womb.

(LUKE 1:42)

WHAT YOU NEED

Mother Mary's Birthday Cake worksheet
Birthday Cake Decorations worksheet
crayons/markers
scissors
glue sticks

PREPARATION

1. Make one copy per child of Mother Mary's Birthday Cake worksheet and Birthday Cake Decorations worksheet.

CRAFT TIME

1. Hand each child a copy of Mother Mary's Birthday Cake worksheet and the Birthday Cake Decorations worksheet.
2. Color the various birthday decorations on the Birthday Cake Decorations worksheet.
3. Cut out each individual decoration.
4. Glue each individual decoration onto the Birthday Cake worksheet.
5. Sing "Happy Birthday" to Mary as you share the decorated cake with your friends!

Mother Mary's Birthday Cake

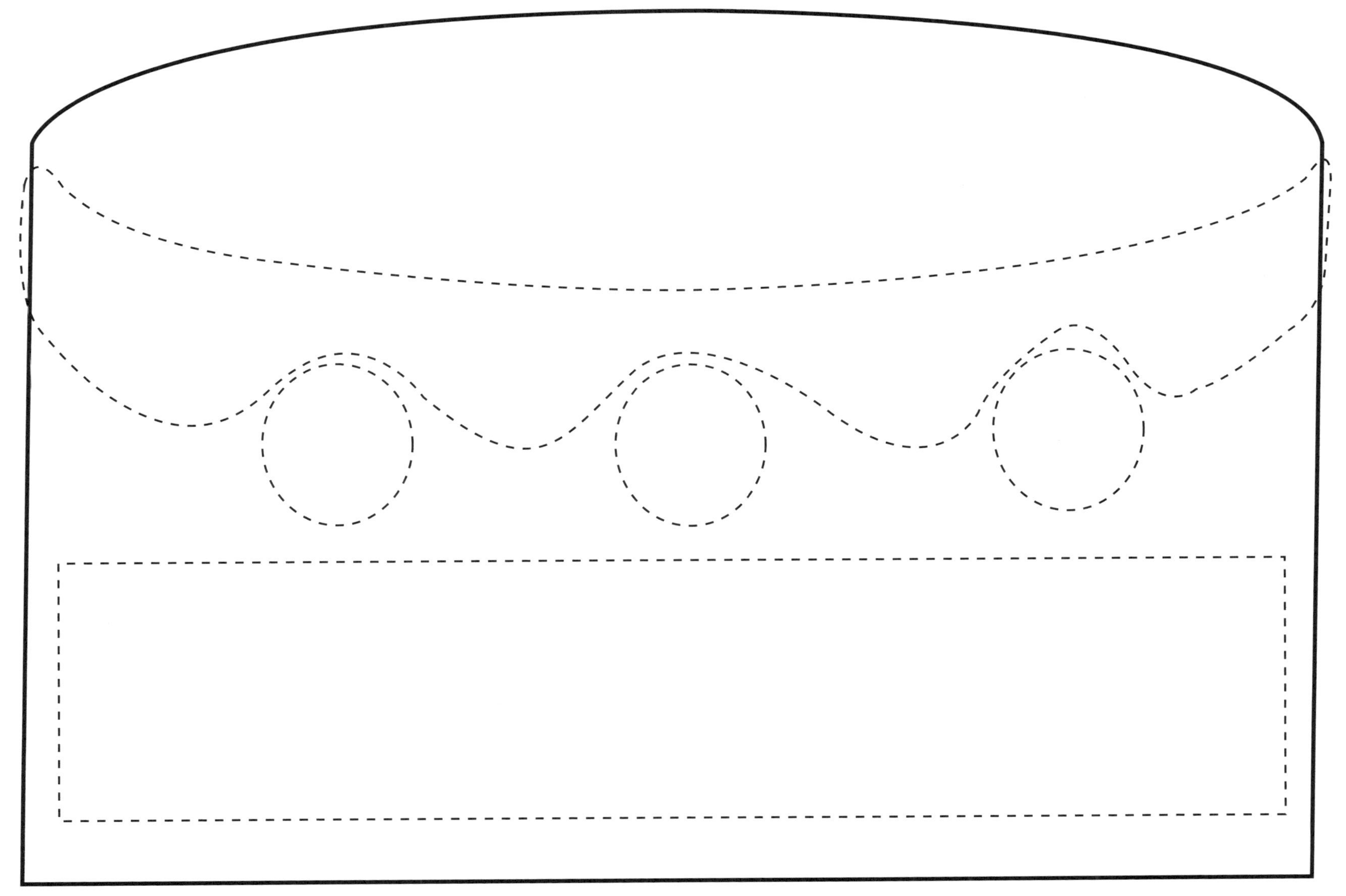

Birthday Cake Decorations

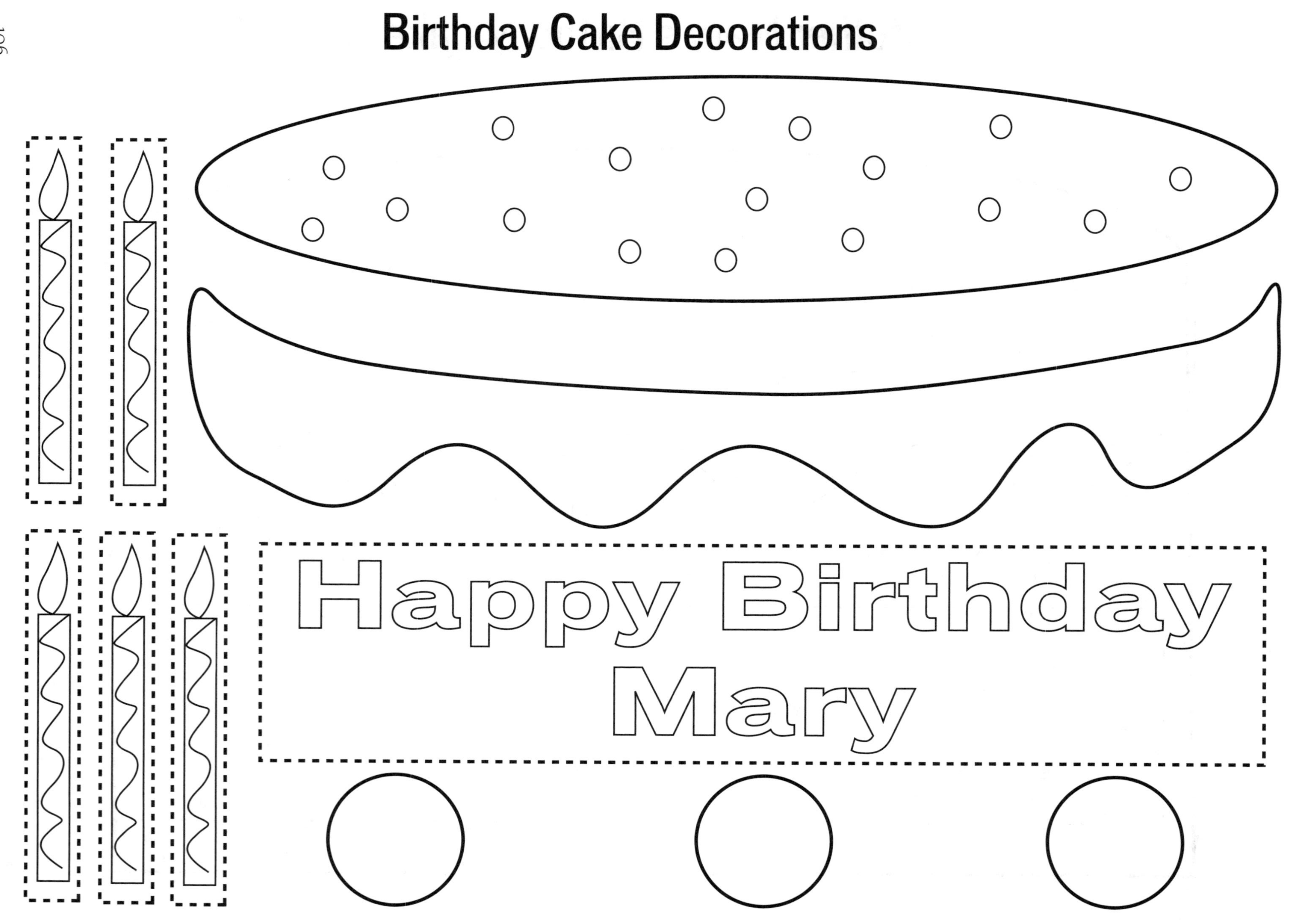

ACTIVITY #27

My Wheel of Saints

Do you know what a saint is? A saint is a person who lived just as God would like all people to live. Saints are very holy and blessed. They have shown extreme love and kindness to many people. Every saint represents something that was very special to them while they lived on Earth. There are saints that represent children, animals, soldiers—just about anything you can think of. Let's make a spinning wheel of saints and learn about the lives of some really special people.

This is my commandment, that you love one another as I have loved you.

(JOHN 15:12)

WHAT YOU NEED

white paper

My Wheel of Saints worksheets (#1 and #2)

exacto knife

scissors

brass paper fasteners

PREPARATION

1. Make one copy per child of My Wheel of Saints worksheets #1 and #2 onto the paper.
2. Using your exacto knife, cut a small hole (directly over the black circle) in the center of each of the wheels.

CRAFT TIME

1. Give each child a copy of My Wheel of Saints worksheets #1 and #2 and one brass paper fastener.
2. Cut out each wheel.
3. Cut out the wedge shape at the top of worksheet #1.
4. Place the wheel you cut out from worksheet #1 on top of the other wheel. Fasten together with the brass paper fastener.
5. Spin the wheel and learn about the saints!

My Wheel of Saints #1

My Wheel of Saints #2

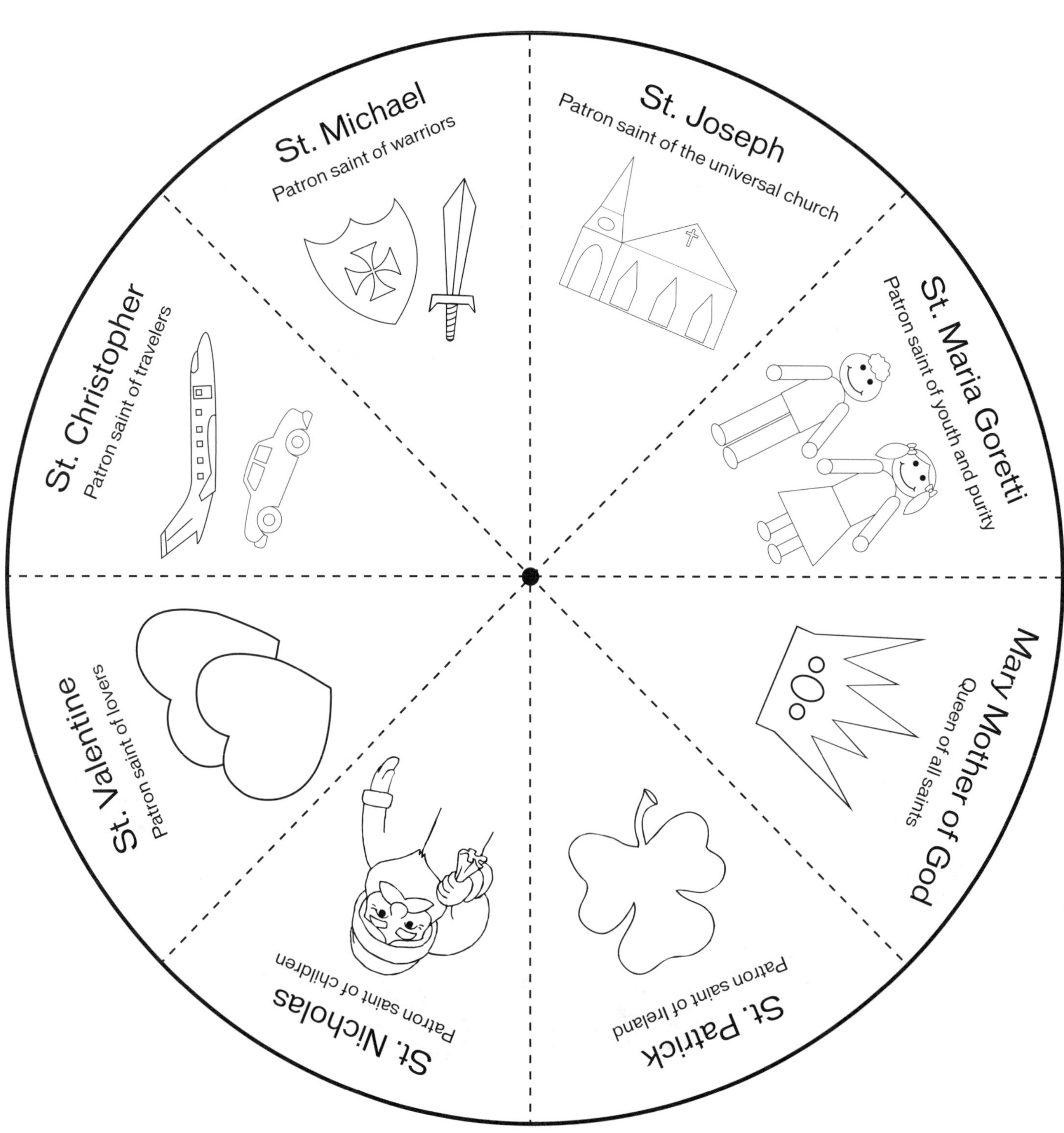

ACTIVITY #28

Thanksgiving Corn Magnet/Key Chain

Thanksgiving is a special holiday when we give thanks for the abundance of wonderful things in our lives. We can thank God for our toys, the rain, our food, and our family and friends. In many ways we are just like the Native Americans and the Pilgrims: We need to help each other in order to appreciate and participate in the abundant feast of life.
Let us make a wonderful Thanksgiving corn project to remind us of the abundance that God provides for us each and every day!

O give thanks to the Lord,
for he is good;
his steadfast love
endures forever!

(PSALMS 118:1)

WHAT YOU NEED

brown or tan pipe cleaners (one per child)

harvest colored tri-beads (red, orange, yellow, gold, clear, white, brown)

raffia

scissors

glue (tacky or hot) (*optional*)

magnet or key chain ring (*optional*)

PREPARATION

1. Begin by cutting the pipe cleaners into two 6" pieces.
2. Cut raffia into 6" pieces.
3. Assemble kits.

   Each kit should include: two 6" pipe cleaners, raffia, thirty-three multicolored beads, and optional magnet or key chain ring.

CRAFT TIME

1. Give each child one pre-assembled kit.
2. Form an "X" using two 6" pipe cleaners.
3. Wrap one of the pipe cleaner's legs around the center of the "X" two times. Next, bend the pipe cleaners to form the shape of a chicken's foot.

   The shortest cleaner will be the stem of the corn.

4. String eleven multicolored beads onto each of the longest pipe cleaners. Bend the end of the cleaner to secure beads in place.
5. Tie the raffia tightly around the short stem of the corn.
6. *Optional*: Glue the magnet to the back of the corn, or fasten the key chain ring through the raffia to complete the project.
7. Enjoy or give to a friend who you are thankful for!

ACTIVITY #29

My Advent Wreath

Long ago, a beautiful baby boy was born. He was born in a manger filled with animals and hay, and a star shone bright in the sky. That baby boy brought to Earth a light that cleared out all the darkness. The light that he brought has never gone out.

Jesus Christ was that baby, and he is the reason why Christmas is such a special time. Jesus is the reason why we just can't stop ourselves from smiling a little bit bigger, laughing a little bit louder, and loving just a little bit more.

Let's sit down with our family and friends and create a beautiful Advent wreath in the tradition of this wonderful season. Let the beauty and the light of the wreath shine brightly. It will remind you of the love that Jesus has for us all! Whenever you like—at dinner, snack time, or anytime—say a prayer to reflect upon the love and light of Christ.

Again Jesus spoke to them, saying, "I am the light of the world. Whoever follows me will never walk in darkness but will have the light of life."

(JOHN 8:12)

WHAT YOU NEED

Advent Wreath handout
paper plates (one per child)
scissors
green tissue paper
red tissue paper
glue sticks
large gum drops
plastic knife
birthday candles
(three purple and one pink)

PREPARATION

1. Begin by cutting a hole in the center of the paper plate. The hole should be large enough to leave a 2" rim around the plate.
2. Cut green and red tissue paper into 1" x 1" pieces.
3. Assemble kits.
   Each kit should include: one plate, four gum drops, three purple candles, and one pink candle.

CRAFT TIME

1. Give each child one pre-assembled kit.
2. Place a mound of green and red tissue paper in the center of the table.
3. Begin by covering one-tenth of the paper plate with glue.
4. Place your pointer finger into the center of one of the squares of tissue paper. Pull the edges up around your finger to resemble a cup.
5. Immediately place your finger with the tissue paper downward onto the glued portion of the plate.
6. Repeat Steps 3 through 5 until entire plate is covered and no white is showing.
7. Using your plastic knife, slice off a thin layer of the bottom of the gumdrop.
8. Space the gumdrops evenly around the wreath and gently push the sticky side of the gumdrop onto the plate until firm.
9. Push each of the four candles into the center of the four gumdrops.
10. Light the candles and say a prayer!

The Advent Wreath

Happy Advent! Today in class we learned all about the season of Advent. In celebration of this wonderful season, we made Advent wreaths for the children to share with their families at home.

The Advent wreath is time-honored tradition in the Catholic Church. During this special time of the year, we reflect on the fact that Christ is "the light of the world" and that he came to take away the darkness of sin and to illuminate us with the truth and love of God (John 3:19–21).

The Advent wreath has beautiful symbolism and is a useful tool in sharing the true meaning of Christmas with children young and old. Below we have listed the meanings of the wreath and candles. Please enjoy this wreath during the season of Advent and remember to reflect upon the love and the light of Christ!

Happy Advent and Merry Christmas!

CIRCULAR WREATH MADE OF PINE OR HOLLY LEAVES

The circular wreath has no beginning or end, which symbolizes God's eternity and the everlasting life he brought to us when he came to deliver us from our sins. The prickly spikes of the pine or holly leaves represent the crown of thorns. The green symbolizes life and resurrection.

THE CANDLES

Each of the four candles represents the four weeks of Advent. Tradition holds that each week represents one thousand years, adding up to the 4,000 years from Adam and Eve until the birth of Jesus Christ. Three of the candles are purple and one is pink.

PURPLE CANDLE (WEEK 1)

Purple is a symbol of royalty, so we use this color to signify the coming of the King. The first week's candle also signifies hope.

PURPLE CANDLE (WEEK 2)

Again, purple is a symbol of royalty, signifying the coming of the King. The second week's candle represents love.

PINK CANDLE (WEEK 3)

The third candle is pink like the rose-colored vestments the priest wears at Mass on the Third Sunday of Advent. This Sunday is called Gaudete Sunday. The pope used to hand out roses on the third Sunday to the faithful. This signified joy and therefore the third candle is pink. The third week's candle also represents joy.

PURPLE CANDLE (WEEK 4)

The final candle is again purple, signifying the coming of the King. The fourth week's candle represents peace.

ACTIVITY #30

Snowflakes From Heaven

Have you ever seen a snowflake? Have you ever thought about what they look like? Sure, they are all white, small, and wet, but each of them is very different. Some snowflakes are big, fat, and really wet, and others are tiny and feel like powder against your face. In many ways, humans are like snowflakes. When God made each of us, he made parts of us similar and parts of us different. Just like snowflakes, every person is a different size and shape, and yet we are all beautiful in our unique way. Today we'll make a snowflake to show the beauty that lies within us all!

Honor and majesty are before him; strength and beauty are in his sanctuary.

(PSALMS 96:6)

WHAT YOU NEED

Small or Large Snowflake template

scissors

glue stick

glitter

plastic container, medium-sized (large enough to place a finished snowflake flat inside)

PREPARATION

1. Make copies of the Snowflake templates. One per child is needed.

CRAFT TIME

1. Cut out the snowflake template.
2. Fold in half.

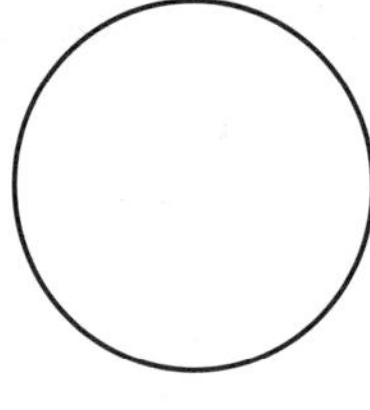

Step 1

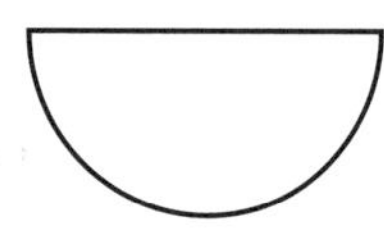

Step 2

3. Fold the paper in half again. Repeat one more time.

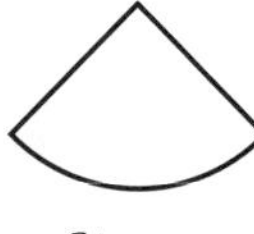

Step 3

Step 4

4. Cut patterns on the folded sides. Be careful not to cut all the way to the other side or your snowflake will be cut in half. Experiment using different types of patterns.

5. Unfold the patterned snowflake.
6. Gently rub glue onto the snowflake.
7. Place snowflake in plastic container and sprinkle with glitter.
8. Enjoy!

ACTIVITY #31

The Three Wise Men– A Wise Choice

The Bible is the most interesting and colorful book of all time. We all love to hear a good story, so it's a great idea to read the stories that help us learn about Jesus and his life, so that we might further grow together in God's love. One great story is the story of the Three Wise Men and the special choice that they made. Let's read together the story of these three kings in Matthew 2:1–12 and think and imagine what it must have been like to travel such a distance following a star!

WHAT YOU NEED

- The Three Wise Men worksheets (#1 and #2)
- glue
- scissors

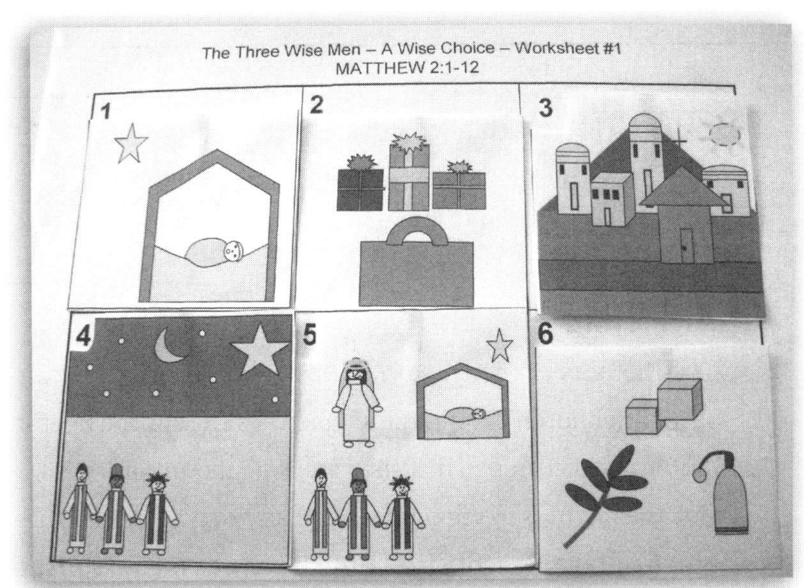

Jesus was born in the town of Bethlehem. During that time, King Herod was the ruler. Soon after the birth of baby Jesus, Three Wise Men came from the east and asked, "Where is the baby who has been born King of the Jews? We saw his star in the east, and have come to worship him."

When the king heard this, he became very upset, along with all the people in Jerusalem. So he gathered all the chief priests and scribes and asked them where Jesus was to be born, and they told him Bethlehem.

Next, King Herod called the Three Wise Men to a secret meeting and found out when the star had appeared. He told the Wise Men, "Go to Bethlehem and find the baby, and when you find him, let me know, so that I can worship him too."

And so the Wise Men left, and on their trip they saw the same star they had seen in the East. The sight of the star gave them great joy, because they knew it would lead them to Jesus. They continued to follow the star until they came to the place where Jesus was.

They went into the house, and saw the child with his Mother Mary, and they knelt down to worship him. They gave him gifts of gold, frankincense, and myrrh.

The Wise Men returned to their country by another road because God warned them in a dream not to go back to King Herod.

(BASED ON MATTHEW 2:1–12)

PREPARATION

1. Make one copy per child of worksheets #1 and #2.

CRAFT TIME

1. Read the story of the Three Wise Men (found in Matthew 2:1–12) to the children.
2. Have the children cut out the six pictures from worksheet #2.
3. Shuffle the pictures so that they are in a random order.
4. Glue the pictures in sequential order as you go through the story again, making sure to put the right event in the right place. ***Hint: What was the very first thing to happen? – What happened on Christmas Day?***
5. Have fun retelling the story again by looking at the pictures.

The Three Wise Men –A Wise Choice (Matthew 2:1-12)

1	2	3
PASTE HERE	PASTE HERE	PASTE HERE
4	**5**	**6**
PASTE HERE	PASTE HERE	PASTE HERE

The Three Wise Men #2

ACTIVITY #32

Valentine Flower Craft

Have you ever heard the story of St. Valentine? This is a story for all ages. It is one that tells of hard choices, good conquering evil, and, most importantly, love. Valentine lived in Ancient Rome, under an emperor named Claudius II. This evil ruler mandated that no one should marry and that all marriages were null and void because he needed volunteers to fight in a war. He was sure that nobody wanted to be a soldier because all the men wanted to stay home with the ones they loved.

Because Valentine was a devout Christian, he believed that the emperor was wrong and he decided to do what was right under God's law. He knew that he might get in trouble, but he continued to marry young couples in secret. One day the emperor discovered his disobedience and ordered him caught and jailed. During his sentence, many people rallied around Valentine and threw gifts of flowers and notes to his jail cell. They believed in Valentine, and they believed that love could not be outlawed. When the soldiers finally took Valentine away to kill him on February 14, 270, he left a goodbye note for the jailkeeper's daughter, who was one of his dear friends. He signed the note "Love from your Valentine." Today we celebrate this triumph of love over evil by giving those we care about little tokens of affection, and valentines in remembrance of a man who chose to believe in the one true thing that matters, love.

We love because God first loved us.

(1 JOHN 4:19)

WHAT YOU NEED

Petal handout
Leaf worksheet
chenille stems (one per flower)
Hershey's Kisses® (one per flower)
glue gun
tissue paper
green paper
scissors

PREPARATION

1. Start by bending the chenille stem in half. Place glue on the bottom side of one Hershey's Kiss. Immediately place on the round end of the chenille stem to adhere. Hold in place for a few seconds and cool completely.
2. Cut six pieces of 5" x 7" tissue paper per flower.
3. Copy the attached Petal handout on green paper. Cut out individual petals, making sure that each child has one that says "To and From," and another that has the Scripture verse on it.
4. Punch a hole into the left-hand side of each "To and From" petal. Punch another hole into the right-hand side of each Scripture verse petal.
5. Assemble kits.
   Each kit should include: one chenille stem with Hershey's Kiss® attached, six sheets of tissue paper, one "To and From" petal, and one Scripture verse petal.

CRAFT TIME

1. Give each child a kit.
2. Stack tissue paper into one pile.
3. Fold the tissue paper lengthwise like a fan. Younger children can simply gather the tissue paper in the middle and crunch it up for added body.
4. Tie the chenille stem tightly around the tissue paper, making sure that the Hershey's Kiss is directly in the center.
5. Carefully pull out each piece of tissue paper to form the petals. Fluff the flower so that the petals fully surround the Hershey's Kiss.
6. Using scissors, randomly cut little slits in the petals for added texture.
7. On the leaf cutouts, fill in the blanks under "To" and "From."
8. With the typing facing upward, pull one of the "To and From" and Scripture verse cutouts through the bottom of the chenille stems. Each stem should hold one leaf.
9. Once the leaves are on the stems, twist the stems together to insure that the leaves do not fall off.

Leaf Cutouts

ACTIVITY #33

We Remember–The Stations of the Cross Craft

At Easter we come together to remember the wonderful gift that Jesus gave us. We remember his deep love for us, as well as his suffering in this world. As we walk through the fourteen Stations of the Cross, Jesus' love is even further revealed. Let's walk together on this sometimes sad but always miraculous journey.

The angel said to the women, "Do not be afraid; I know that you are looking for Jesus who was crucified. He is not here; for he has been raised, as he said. Come, see the place where he lay. Then go quickly and tell his disciples, 'He has been raised from the dead, and indeed he is going ahead of you to Galilee; there you will see him.'"

(MATTHEW 28:5–7)

WHAT YOU NEED

Cross worksheets (#1 and #2) (one per child)
Stations of the Cross cutouts (one per child)
Stations of the Cross handout
8" x 10" colored paper (one per child)
8" x 10" white paper (one per child)
scissors
hole punch
string or yarn
glue or glue stick
crayons or markers (*optional*)

PREPARATION

1. Copy page 1 of the Cross worksheet onto colored paper. Next, copy page 2 of the Cross worksheet onto the back of page 1 to make a double-sided cross.
2. Cut out the double-sided cross.
3. Punch a hole at the top of the cross.
4. Cut a strand of yarn approximately 7" long. Tie the yarn onto the cross. This will be used to hang or display the Stations.
5. Copy the Stations of the Cross worksheet onto the plain white paper.
6. Cut out each of the fourteen Stations of the Cross.
7. Make kits by paper clipping the fourteen Stations to the top of the cross.

CRAFT TIME

1. Give each child a craft kit.
2. Starting with the number 1, match each Station (the numbers are in the upper right-hand corner) to the corresponding number on the cross.
3. Paste each Station onto the appropriate square.
4. Discuss each Station and contemplate on how Jesus must have felt as he made his journey. Use the handout to facilitate discussion.
5. If desired, color the Stations.

Stations of the Cross handout

We are pilgrims of the New Age. Let's take a journey together to the land where Jesus sacrificed for our freedom from sin. Let's walk with Jesus on his long journey to resurrection. Below you will find a list of questions and comments that correspond with the fourteen Stations of the Cross. You can visit all fourteen Stations at once, or you can visit just one a day and reflect and pray on it.

STATION 1: JESUS IS CONDEMNED TO DEATH

People are yelling and screaming "Crucify him!" These are the same people who exalted Jesus a week earlier, lining the streets with palms. These people yell and scream horrible things to Jesus. They tell lies and spit in his face. How do you think Jesus felt? Has anybody ever told things that were not true about you? How did it make you feel?

STATION 2: JESUS CARRIES THE CROSS

Jesus is ordered to carry a cross that is heavier and larger than he is. He asks God to help him because he knows he has a long road ahead. Jesus did not want to carry the cross, but he knew he had to do it to save us from our sins. Have you ever had to do something you didn't want to do? Did you do it anyway? Did you ask anyone for help?

STATION 3: JESUS FALLS THE FIRST TIME

The cross is so heavy it is almost impossible to bear. Jesus has no shoes on, so the rocks on the ground begin to cut into his feet. The soldiers are yelling at him to continue. Jesus falls to the ground in angst. He is tired and weary, so he cries up to his heavenly Father for help. Have you ever fallen so hard that you didn't want to get up? What made you find the courage to get up again?

STATION 4: JESUS MEETS HIS MOTHER

Along his walk, Jesus comes upon his mother. She is so sad to see him suffer. He is equally sad to see the pain on her face. They both understand the road that is ahead, and they know that God will help them through this pain. Yet it is still very hard for them.

Have you ever known anyone who was going through a difficult time in their life? Did it make you sad to see them go through such a hard time? Do you think it made them feel better to have you there?

STATION 5: SIMON HELPS JESUS CARRY THE CROSS

Jesus is very tired. The load of the cross is too much to bear. The soldiers stop and pan the crowd for someone who is big and strong and can help Jesus carry the cross. They see Simon and tell him to help Jesus. Simon takes up the cross, and Jesus whispers "Thank you." In the midst of all his pain, Jesus feels bad for Simon. Jesus wants to carry the cross all by himself, but cannot. He has to let someone else help. Have you ever helped someone who was having a hard time? Was it something you wanted to do? Sometimes helping others can be hard. Can you think of a time when helping someone was a hard choice to make?

STATION 6: VERONICA WIPES JESUS' FACE

Jesus is still tired, hot, and very dusty. A woman named Veronica worries for Jesus, so she moves to the front of the crowd and tries to help cool him off. She wipes a clean cloth across his face, hoping it will help a little.

Jesus is so thankful to her that he leaves an impression of his face on her cloth. Have you ever done something small for someone to help make them feel better? Maybe you made them a card or gave them something to drink. Sometimes the little things we do each day mean the most.

STATION 7: JESUS FALLS THE SECOND TIME

Jesus is growing even more tired. He falls again. He doesn't want to get up, but he does. He continues to ask the Lord to help him. Have you ever tried to do something that was hard, and you thought you couldn't do it? Did you have to try many times without success? What made you keep trying?

STATION 8: JESUS MEETS WOMEN WHO ARE CRYING

On his journey, Jesus comes across some women who are crying for him. Although he is in pain and very tired, he is worried about the women. He tells them not to cry for him. He tells them to stay strong and to take care of one another and their children. During his deepest pain, Jesus is worried about others. Sometimes it is easier to think of ourselves and how we feel. We must always remember other people and consider their feelings. Have you ever wondered how others were feeling when you were in pain?

STATION 9: JESUS FALLS A THIRD TIME

Jesus is completely tired. Yet, he goes on. He falls for a third time, with his face in the dirt and that heavy cross on his back. He summons all the strength he has to go on. He prays deeply and fervently for God's help. Patiently and continuously he prays. Have you ever prayed to God for help? Did you continue to pray even when you felt like your goal was very far away?

STATION 10: JESUS IS STRIPPED OF HIS CLOTHES

Jesus finally reaches the end of his long walk with the cross. The soldiers continue to yell and call him names. They are trying to humiliate him and break his spirit so they remove his clothes. They leave a small loincloth for him to wear around his waist. Has anyone ever said something mean to you to make you mad or sad? How did you react? We should ask God to give us the strength to be strong when others try to bring us down.

STATION 11: JESUS IS NAILED TO THE CROSS

The soldiers nail Jesus to the cross. The pain is unbearable, but Jesus continues to be strong in God. Jesus says "Forgive them, Father, for they know not what they do." Have you ever forgiven somebody who tried to hurt you? Why or why not?

STATION 12: JESUS DIES ON THE CROSS

The sky turns dark and the earth quakes as God shows his displeasure. Jesus dies on the cross as Mary watches and cries. His earthly pain is now over; for that she is grateful.

STATION 13: JESUS IS TAKEN DOWN FROM THE CROSS

Jesus' friends take him down from the cross and wrap him in clean linens. Mary and all those who loved him are so sad that he is gone. They miss Jesus already, but they know that he will go on to rise from the dead and live with God in heaven forever. Have you ever moved away from a friend or lost a special pet? How did you feel? How did you get over it?

STATION 14: JESUS IS BURIED

Jesus is carried by his loved ones to a cave where he is buried. A large stone is placed in front of the opening so that his body can rest in peace. Jesus will soon rise from the dead and fulfill his promise of a new life in Christ. Jesus saves us all through his good works. Have you ever done something difficult that ended with you helping others out? Were you acting in the image of Jesus?

Cross #1

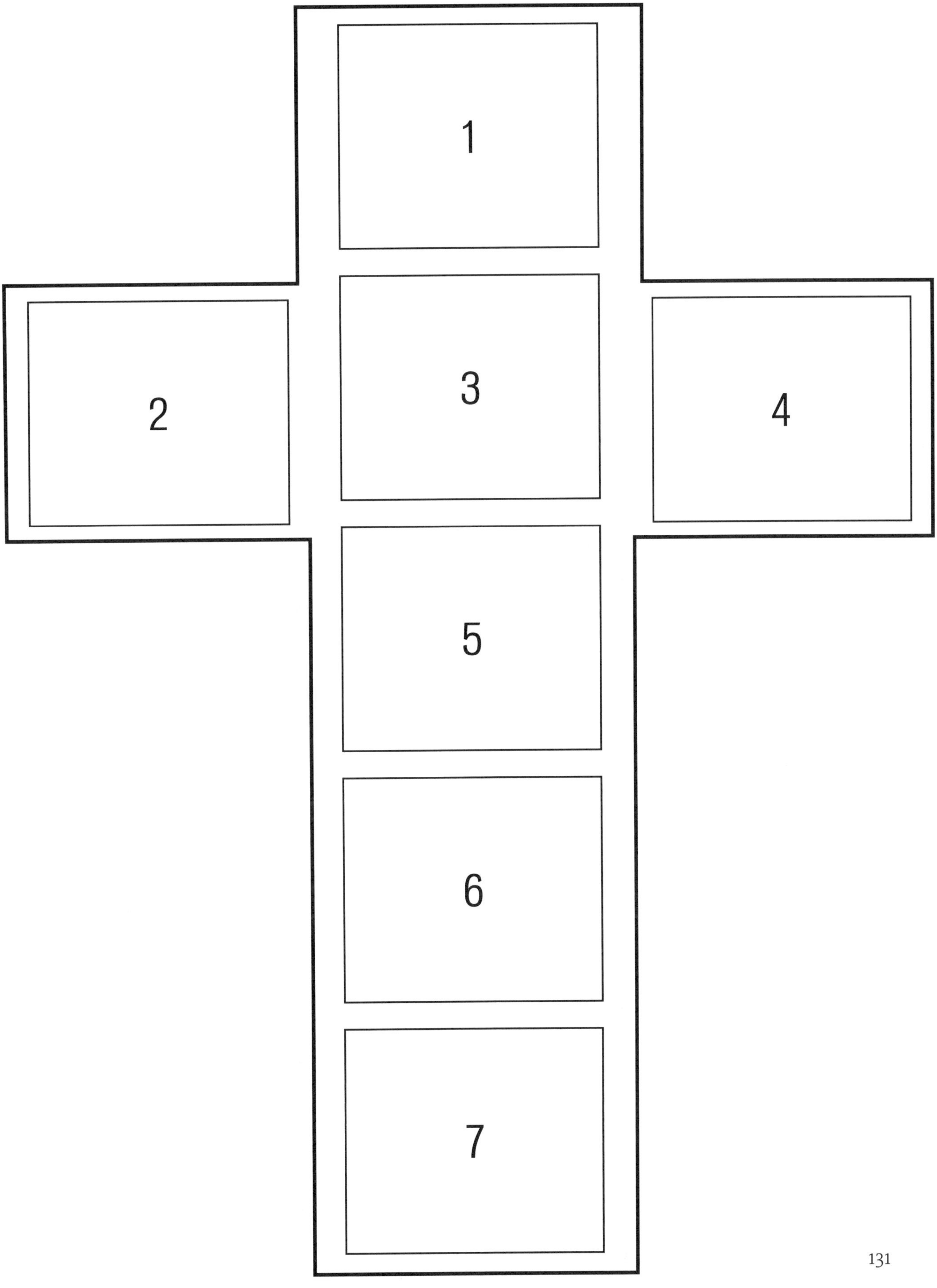

1

2

3

4

5

6

7

Cross #2

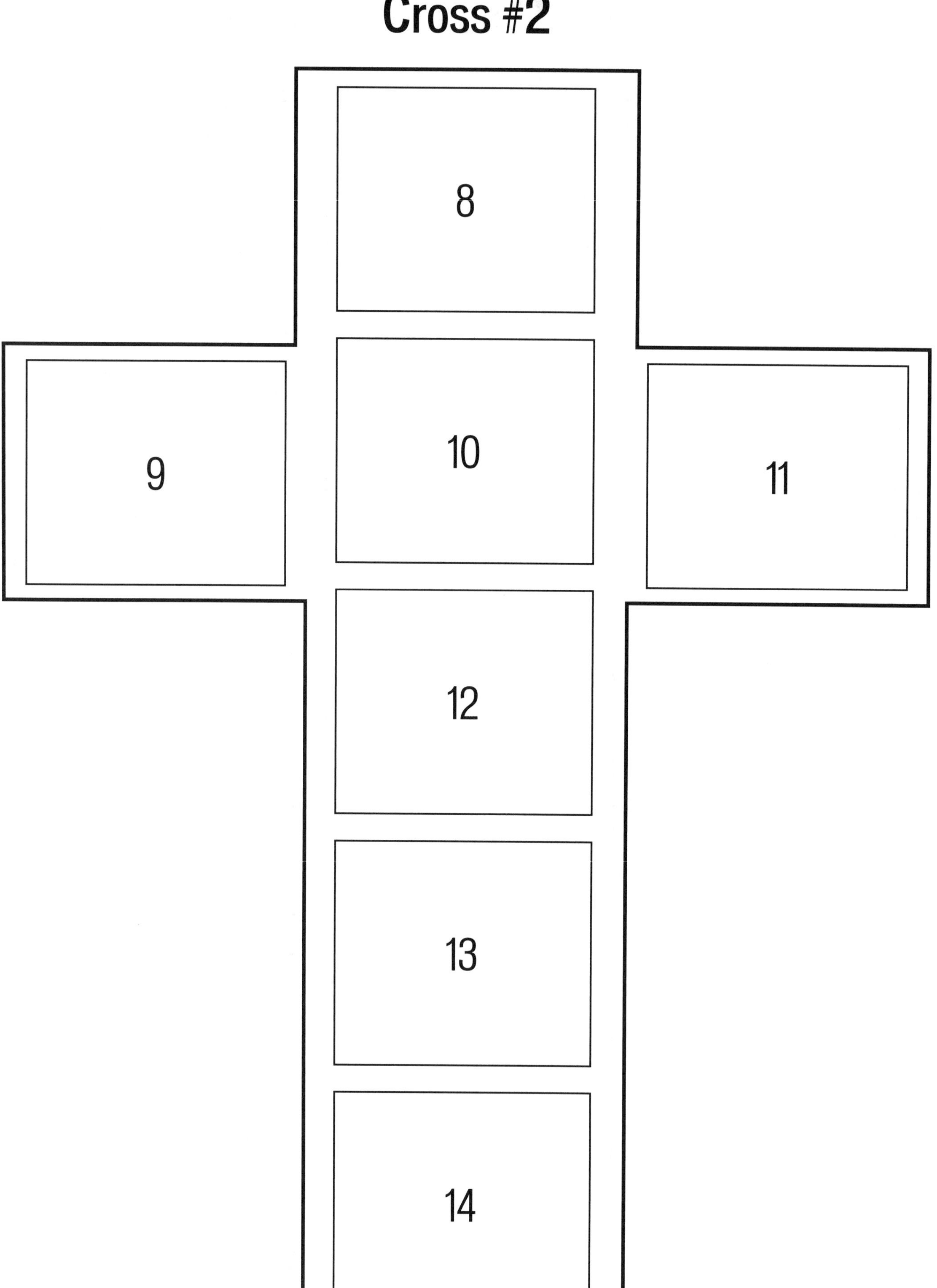

Stations of the Cross

1

Jesus is condemned to death.

2

Jesus carries the cross.

3

Jesus falls the first time.

4

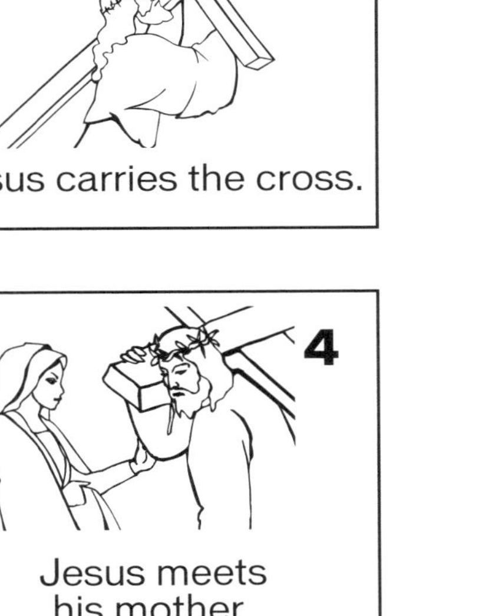

Jesus meets his mother.

5

Simon helps Jesus carry the cross.

6

Veronica wipes Jesus' face.

7

Jesus falls the second time.

8

Jesus meets women who are crying.

9

Jesus falls a third time.

10

Jesus' clothes are taken away.

11

Jesus is nailed to the cross.

12

Jesus dies on the cross.

13

Jesus is taken down from the cross.

14

Jesus is buried.

ACTIVITY #34

Saint Joseph–A Good Caregiver Award

Do you know what a caregiver is? A caregiver is someone who looks after another person. A caregiver can be a mom, dad, grandparent, cousin, friend, or even a teacher. St. Joseph was a caregiver, too. He took care of Jesus and Mary, the Holy Family. Let's make an award for the special caregivers in our lives. We want them to know just how much we love them.

WHAT YOU NEED

- Good Caregiver Award worksheet
- scissors
- ribbons
- crayons/markers
- stapler

For I have set you an example, that you also should do as I have done to you.

(JOHN 13:15)

PREPARATION

1. Make desired number of copies of the Good Caregiver Award worksheet. Cut worksheet in half. Each half will be one award/badge.
2. Cut ribbon into 4" long pieces.
3. Assemble kits.
   Each kit should include: one Good Caregiver Award badge and two 4" ribbons.

CRAFT TIME

1. Give each child one pre-assembled kit.
2. Color the badges using crayons and markers.
3. In the space provided, write to whom the award will be given.
4. Carefully cut out the badge.
5. Staple ribbon to the bottom of the badge and award someone you love!

Good Caregiver Award

ACTIVITY #35

Easter Woven Basket Craft and New Life Hunt

What are the things that remind you of Easter? Every year when Lent arrives we start seeing signs of new life everywhere—little baby bunnies hopping around, newly formed flowers in the garden, green grass, and much more. Why do these things remind us of Easter? Maybe it is because they are all signs of the new life that we have through the Resurrection of Christ. We have such an abundance and so much to be thankful for in the Lord. Let's praise God and all his goodness today and make an Easter basket that symbolizes our abundance of joy, faith, love, and, most importantly, life. Now we will live forever, for Jesus has risen! When you're done making your spectacular basket, maybe someone will hide some wonderful reminders of the new life you have in Christ, just for you to find! Have fun!

Therefore we have been buried with him by baptism into death, so that, just as Christ was raised from the dead by the glory of the Father, so we too might walk in newness of life.

(ROMANS 6:4)

WHAT YOU NEED

Easter Basket Template worksheet
Basket Handle worksheet
Longer Side Weave Strips worksheet
Shorter Side Weave Strips worksheet
colored paper (two different colors)
scissors
exacto knife
glue sticks

PREPARATION

1. Make one copy per child of the Easter Basket Template worksheet onto the colored paper.
2. Cut out each template.
3. Make copies of the Basket Handle, Longer Side Weave Strips, and Shorter Side Weave Strips worksheets on your second color of paper.
4. Cut out one handle, five long strips, and two short strips per basket.
5. Assemble kits.
   Each kit should include: one Easter Basket Template, one Handle cutout, five Long Strips cutouts, and two Shorter Strips cutouts.

CRAFT TIME

1. Using a glue stick, put a small amount of glue over the dotted lines.
2. Place your long weave strips on the longer lines, and place your short weave strips on the shorter lines.
3. Place glue over all the tabs that indicate "GLUE."
4. To make the basket form, fold each side upward on the solid lines.
5. Affix the "GLUE" tab to the appropriate side to seal closed.
6. Glue or staple the basket handle to the sides of the basket to complete your Easter craft!

New Life Hunt

Springtime is the perfect time to see signs of new life. Take a look outside and gather up some things that remind you of your "new life" in Christ. Once you find the items, have someone hide them and go on a New Life Hunt.

Here's a list of things we used in our hunt:

- wildflowers tied together with ribbon
- leaves of different sizes and shapes
- two sticks tied together to form a cross
- bag of soil
- feathers
- acorns or other seeds
- grass tied together in a bouquet
- pebbles painted like ladybugs

Basket Template

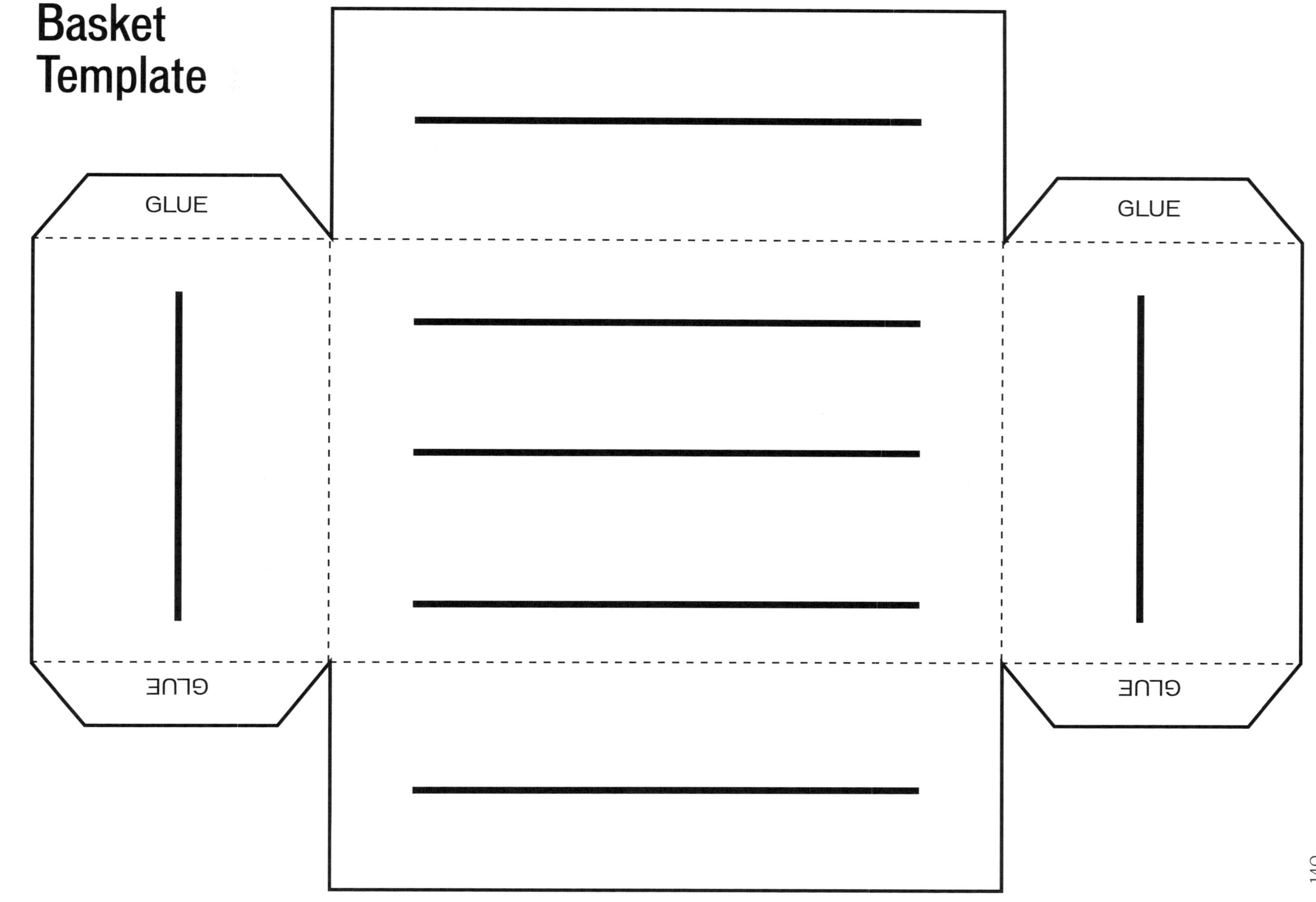

Handle / Long and Short Weave Strips

ACTIVITY #36

Remembering Mother Mary–Mother's Day Craft

Mothers are special, there's no doubt about that! They love us, nurture us, and help us to grow in the Holy Spirit. The Blessed Virgin Mary was the mother of Jesus, and he loved her very much. Mary loved Jesus, too. Did you know that she also has that same love for you and me? Let's pay tribute to Mary and our own mothers by making them a picture frame adorned with many beautiful things we find in nature like flowers, butterflies, and ladybugs. We will give them a gift of natural beauty, much like the beauty they give to us each and every day.

Mother—
Her children arise and call her blessed.

(BASED ON PROVERBS 31:28)

WHAT YOU NEED

Mother Scripture / Daisy / Butterfly worksheet
business-size envelopes
8" x 10" typing paper
colored typing paper (five different colors)
popsicle sticks
colored tissue paper (two pieces of 2 ½" x 4" and two pieces of 1" x 4")
pistachio shells (*optional*)
pom-poms (*optional*)
red and black markers
exacto knife or scissors
glue stick
tape
photograph (*optional*)

****Note: If using a photograph of each child, request that each parent bring in a recent photo of his/her child the week prior to the craft. Another option is to take digital pictures of the children and print them out for classroom use.***

PREPARATION

1. Cut a large rectangular hole in the center of the front side of the envelope. The hole should be slightly smaller than your picture.
2. Using the typing paper, cut one 5" x 2½" piece of paper per picture frame. Fold the ends upward (along the dotted lines in the diagram) about 1" inward from the end of the paper.

3. Tape a popsicle stick to the inside of the envelope flap (see below). This will be used as the stand to hold the picture frame up.

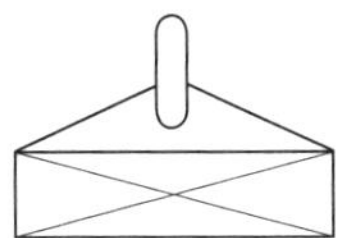

4. Using the tissue paper, cut out two 2½" x 4" sheets per picture frame. Next, cut out two 1" x 4" sheets per picture frame.

5. Copy or print the Daisy worksheet onto two different colored sheets of typing paper. Cut out two daisies per picture frame. If you would like to add further dimension to the picture frame, cut slits around the petals of the daisies and gently lift the petals to varying heights to create a 3D effect.
6. Photocopy or print the Butterfly worksheet onto two different colored sheets of typing paper. Cut out two butterflies per picture frame.
7. If using pistachio shells, color each half shell red with a marker. On one end color the top quarter black. Draw a black line down the middle of the back. Next, make five small dots on each side of the line (see below).

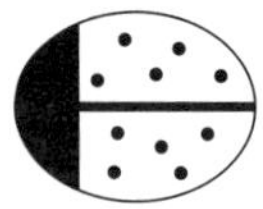

8. Using the fifth color of the typing paper, photocopy or print the Mother's Day Bible Verse onto the typing paper. Cut out one Bible verse per picture frame.
9. Assemble kits.
   Each kit should include: one envelope with hole cut in center and popsicle stick taped to the back, one 5" x 2½" white paper, two 2½" x 4" sheets of tissue paper, two 1" x 4" sheets of tissue paper, two daisies, two pom-poms, two butterflies, four or five ladybugs, and one Bible verse.

CRAFT TIME

1. Hand out pre-assembled kits.
2. Glue the 5" x 2½" white paper to the front of the picture frame. It should be glued to the bottom middle of the envelope, just below the picture frame hole.

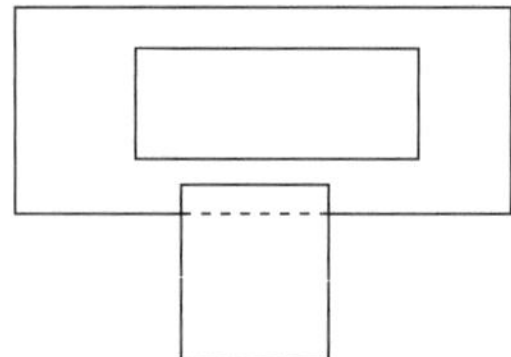

3. Glue the smaller tissue paper pieces above and below the picture frame hole. Next, glue the larger tissue paper pieces to the sides of the picture frame hole.
4. Glue the Bible verse above the picture frame hole, in the upper middle of the picture frame.
5. Glue the daisies onto the frame by only placing glue into the center of the flower. Pull the petals up and apart to add a 3D effect. Glue pom-poms in the center of the daisy for additional detail.
6. Glue only the center of the butterfly onto the frame. Fold the wings upward, so the butterfly appears as if he might fly off the page.
7. Glue the ladybugs onto the frame. If you have a problem keeping them glued down, you may want to glue a little cotton ball into the inside of the shell, and then put glue on the cotton to help it adhere to the frame.
8. Allow the frame to dry for ten minutes before placing a picture inside.

Mother Scripture / Daisy / Butterfly

Happy Mother's Day

Mother –
Her children arise and call her blessed.

BASED ON PROVERBS 31:28

ACTIVITY #37

A Book About My Mom

Moms are a blessing from heaven. They know how to play our favorite games, they bake our favorite cookies, and they love us no matter what. Jesus had a mother too. Her name was Mary. Mary did all the things for Jesus that your mom does for you. She knew his favorite foods, played his favorite games, and taught him all types of things.

Let's put together a book all about our moms, and why they are so special. Then, we'll sit down with our moms, and tell them how much we love them.

Honor your father and mother.

(EXODUS 20:12)

WHAT YOU NEED

- My Mom Book worksheets
- stapler
- crayons/markers

PREPARATION

1. Make copies of My Mom Book worksheets. One per child is needed. First print cover sheet, page 8/1, and page 6/3. Once those pages are printed turn them over and print pages 9, 2/7, and 4/5 on the back, respectively.
2. Place pages in order, fold in half, and staple along the seam.

CRAFT TIME

1. Hand out booklets.
2. Sign the front of the book.
3. Go through each page and finish the sentences about your mom.
4. Draw a picture in the space provided that corresponds to the writing.
5. Share your book with your mom!

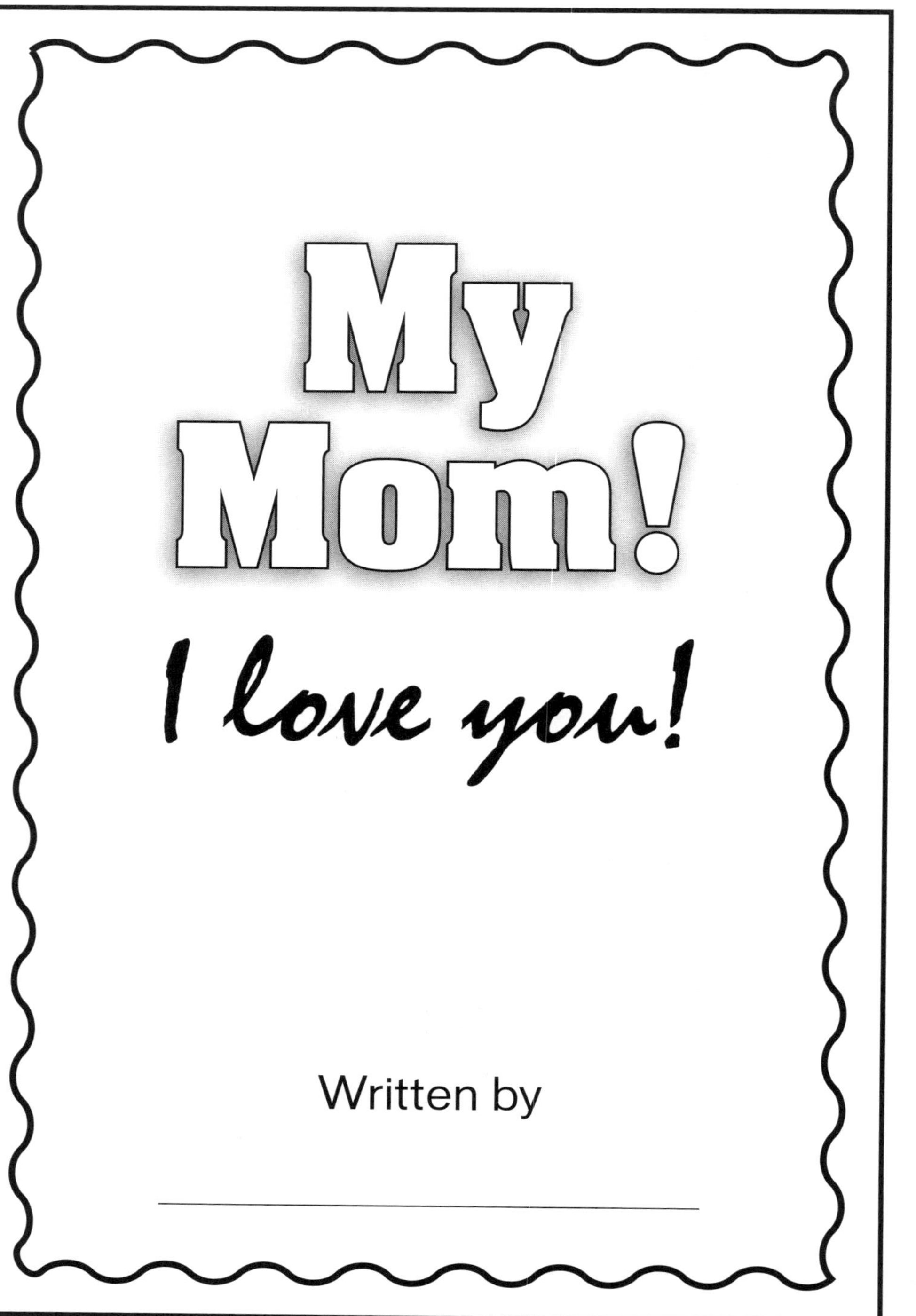
My Mom!
I love you!
Written by

8

The prettiest thing about my mom is

_______________________________.

1

My mom is special because

_______________________________.

6

My mom and I like to eat

________________________.

3

My mom and I like to play

________________________.

9

**Mother–
Her children arise
and call her blessed.**

BASED ON PROVERBS 31

My mom is the best at

______________________.

2

My mom reminds me of
Jesus when

________________________.

7

My mom teaches me about

________________________.

4

My mom and I like to read

________________________.

5

My mom and I have fun when we

________________________.